RELIGIOUS TYRANNY
SPIRITUAL TRUTHS

Alan Seymour

Love & Light

Alan Seymour

Published in 2017 by FeedARead.com Publishing

Copyright © Alan Seymour

First Edition

A CIP catalogue record for this title is available from the British
Library.

Contents

Acknowledgements

I wish to thank the Spiritual Truth Foundation for their kind permission to reproduce some of the text from the Silver Birch publications.

I also give thanks to the Spiritualists' National Union for permission to reproduce definitions of the Seven Principles of Spiritualism.

FOREWORD

Since I was a child I have been fascinated by stories of mystery, the supernatural and things that can be generally thought of as 'unexplained'. Also, when I began to learn about the Christian religion at my infant and then junior school, (at that time Christianity was the only religion taught in my school) I was generally receptive to what I was being taught about the Nativity and so many other stories in the Bible that were taught and explained by the religious education teachers.

To an innocent child who trusted his peers, it seemed to be the right thing to do, to accept the requirements of my teachers to include the Christian religion in our religious education lessons and, after all, who was I to question my elders and betters?

Stories of miracles in the Bible were told by teachers who never allowed themselves to be questioned about the possibility of them being exaggerated or just plain impossible to believe, preferring to disregard any form of dissent which deviated from the religious curriculum, based as it was on the established religion of the United Kingdom. Their vague answers led me to doubt the validity of the teachings. It was as though I was being told to just accept what they were telling me, without question, something I have never felt comfortable with.

To my mind, it is necessary to back up a belief in religion or politics with a reasoned argument so that other points of view can be discussed to enable people to listen and analyse the subject before drawing their own conclusions, without forgetting that it is not wrong to change those conclusions based on the various facts that may become available in the future. To do otherwise means that there is a tendency towards a dogmatic approach which is defined in the Oxford English Dictionary as 'arrogant declaration of opinion'.

I also wondered why, in a country such as India where people in the 1950's were often shown on news bulletins to be hungry, were forbidden to eat beef which was available in abundance. However, I now realise that this was a generally misguided childhood understanding of the Hindu religion.

In my teenage years, I wondered why it was that Catholics were forbidden to use contraception while at the same time in Africa, where Catholicism has a strong presence, children were dying of starvation due, at least partly, to overpopulation which could have been alleviated using contraception. We then had the AIDS epidemic in the 1980's which might have been less severe if contraception was more easily available.

I mention these things to illustrate in some way, how my thoughts on religion developed over many years and led me to reject orthodox religions that to me, appeared to be too dogmatic in their beliefs.

On leaving school and beginning my working life, other interests became more important and my connection with religion was limited to the 'hatch, match and dispatch' aspects of orthodoxy which were a necessary part of a traditional family in the United Kingdom. Religion, I felt, had its place in life but, much to the irritation of the clergy, it was only being used by many people who wanted to be married in church, (because that was what you did), their children Christened, (just in case there was such a place as Hell), and ceremoniously buried or cremated to ensure their place in Heaven.

I also became aware that many people who were members of the various Christian religions, were fearful of contradicting the hierarchy of the church, fearful of questioning the teachings of the Bible and fearful of going to hell if they did not accept the dogmatic teachings of Christianity.

I cannot think of any subject which has not progressed or been updated to suit changes in knowledge or perception, other than religion. For over two thousand years, stories and myths have been built around various individuals and events without any changes, despite there being a wealth of evidence challenging the perceived wisdom of those ancient teachings.

The twentieth century economist, John Maynard Keynes had a way of putting it, when he is alleged to have said,

'When events change, I change my mind. What do you do?
When the facts change, I change my mind. What do you do, sir?
When my information changes, I alter my conclusions. What do you do, sir?
When someone persuades me that I am wrong, I change my mind. What do you do?'

It wasn't long before I began to realise that historically, many of the world's problems were caused, at least in part, by religion. The Crusades of the Middle Ages, sanctioned by the Roman Catholic Church to restore Christian access to the Holy Land which had come under the influence of Islam, is one such example. This appears to have led to the chaotic situation we now have in the modern world, in which there have been atrocities carried out by extremists claiming to represent Christianity and Islam, but who are merely using the religious differences to generate hatred between peoples.

Over time my interest was aroused about stories of life after death and the work of mediums, sometimes through watching television programs and reading books as well as by having occasional conversations with friends and work colleagues.

Perhaps inevitably during my teenage years I and my friends experimented with an Ouija board, managing to frighten the life out of ourselves with immature questions such as 'is there anybody there?' and 'who will be the first to die?'

I have since learned that if you ask for 'anybody' you will get 'anybody' and that without an experienced medium in attendance all sorts of unpleasant things can happen.

The religion of Spiritualism was often mentioned and I became aware of Spiritualist Churches and the work that they do, including Spiritual healing, mediumship, which can reunite people with loved ones who have passed away, and the understanding of Spiritualist philosophy which is based on the Seven Principles of Spiritualism.

Through Spiritualist publications like Psychic World, Two Worlds and Psychic News I learned more about Spiritualism and how there was no dogma attached to its teachings, rather that people were encouraged to ask questions and to only accept that which they felt comfortable with. The religion is based on proof rather than faith and I felt very comfortable with its teachings.

I read many newspaper articles written by Michael Roll, chairman of the Campaign for Philosophical Freedom, which sought to break the controlling power of orthodox religion, who introduced me to the writings of Thomas Paine, 'the most valuable Englishman ever', according to the title of a documentary broadcast by the BBC in 1982 and presented by Kenneth Griffith. The final book written by Thomas Paine was 'The Age of Reason' first published in 1794 after he had been imprisoned in the Bastille during the French Revolution. It sets out to show how the Bible is not the 'word of God' and how, because of the meeting of the Council of Nicæa in 325 AD, many of the stories it contains are contradictory and often not written by the authors whose names are credited to the writings.

After attending Croydon Spiritualist Church since 1987 I was invited to join the committee and became Vice President in 1998.

One day, in 2001 I received a package by post to my church containing three cd's from a man who did not identify himself, who had been a trainee priest requesting that the information contained in those cd's be published so that a wider audience could benefit from his experience in the Catholic Church.

He sets out to explain that the Bible is not the truth and that many of the stories contained within its pages were 'modified' to maintain the church's power over the people.

By using the same books that claim many things to be true, he sets out to prove them to be false.

It is with all the experiences of my life, including many stories I have read that support my opinions, that I have written this book which may upset some people who are committed Christians, but will perhaps open free thinker's minds to the possibility that they have been misled.

Perhaps other people who, like me have questioned many of the things they were taught about religion but have never received satisfactory answers, will learn a little more about religion and the harm it has done to mankind over many centuries, and continues to do.

Modern Spiritualism is said to have begun after events that took place in Hydesville, New York State on 31st. March 1848 and there are many signed statements from residents in the town confirming the validity of the events, but

I would argue that it was the re-emergence of the beliefs that originated over two thousand years ago, and was once the true representation of what religion should be about.

The Seven Principles of Spiritualism were communicated through the mediumship of Emma Hardinge Britten from Robert Owen, the famous philanthropist and co-founder of the Co-operative movement.

They form the basis of Spiritualist philosophy and are presented and explained in chapter 14 of this book.

Throughout this book, I have quoted many of the sayings of Thomas Paine, Albert Einstein and others, along with teachings inspired from the Spirit world, such as Silver Birch, the Spirit guide who communicated through Maurice Barbenell, and my own guide, Fine Feather, whose teachings have been well documented in my first book, 'A Wonderful Spiritual Journey'. These sayings and teachings have been a source of inspiration to me and challenge the reader to decide for themselves how they compare to the teachings of the Bible as analysed by the anonymous trainee priest who went to great lengths to explain how the Bible has misled generations of people.

Before you read this book, I should point out that I do not necessarily accept some of the provocative language used by the trainee priest under the headings, 'Sacrifices are not necessary', Reincarnation & other topics' and 'The Creation', but I do agree with the general purpose of his writings, to reveal the deceitful way that orthodox religion has corrupted the Bible to serve their own purpose.

Also, Spiritualism does not officially recognise reincarnation as it has not been proved in the way that continuity of life after death has been proved repeatedly by mediums throughout the world and over many years.

CHAPTER 1

Whence arose all the horrid assassinations of whole nations of men, women, and infants, with which the Bible is filled; and the bloody persecutions, and tortures unto death and religious wars, that since that time have laid Europe in blood and ashes; whence arose they, but from this impious thing called revealed religion, and this monstrous belief that God has spoken to man? The lies of the Bible have been the cause of the one, and the lies of the Testament of the other.

Thomas Paine

SACRIFICES ARE NOT NECESSARY
(The transcript of the first CD)

God is subtle but he is not malicious.

Albert Einstein

The Old Testament writers claim that their sins are blotted out by sacrifices. This was backed up by the writers of the New Testament who claim that Jesus paid the ultimate price upon the cross for all of mankind's sins and that his sacrifices have taken the place of the animal sacrifices.

Now all a person needs to do is accept that Jesus died upon the cross for his sins and he will be forgiven and get to heaven.

By using the same books that claim these things to be true, I will prove them to be false.

Deuteronomy chapter 5 verse 6 to 22 explains the Ten Commandments in full but at the end of this it says, 'and he added no more, he wrote them upon two tablets of stone and gave them to me'.

Thus, wrote Moses, or so it is claimed.

There you have the laws according to the Old Testament but please note, 'he added no more'.

God gave the Ten Commandments and 'he added no more'.

Therefore, the laws of sacrifices were man's inventions and not the commandments from God.

This will be proved by various writings from the Old and New Testament.

In Psalm 40 verse 6 David says, 'sacrifices and offerings thou dost not desire but thou hast given me an open ear. Burnt offerings and sin offerings thou hast not required'.

And Psalm 51 verse 16 to 17 reads, 'for thou hast no delight in sacrifices, were I to give a burnt offering thou would not be pleased. My sacrifice, oh God, is a broken spirit, a broken and contrite heart, you, God, will not despise'.

David knew the folly and foolishness of burnt offerings.

Even King Solomon knew the foolishness of killing and sacrificing animals.

Proverbs 21 verse 3, 'to do righteousness and justice is more acceptable to the Lord than sacrifices'.

In Ecclesiastes chapter 5 verse 1, Solomon says 'guard your steps when you go to the house of God.

To draw near to listen is better than to offer the sacrifices of fools because they do not know that they are doing evil'.

Solomon is saying that it's evil to kill animals or birds for sacrifice, and that people who do this are fools. Now the fools don't even know that what they are doing is evil. It is better to listen to instruction than to do sacrifices and what instruction is there but the Ten Commandments?

Thou shalt not kill and yet the fools still did it. Yes, this law applies to all life and not just to humans. This will be revealed in the Old Testament later.

Isaiah 1 chapter 1 and then verses 11 to 17, 'what to me is the multitude of your sacrifices says the lord. I have had enough of burnt offerings of rams and the fattened beasts. I do not delight in the blood of bulls or of lambs or of goats. When you come to appear before me all required of you is trampling in my courts. Bring no more vain offerings. Incense is an abomination to me. New moon and Sabbath and the calling of assemblies I cannot endure likewise, and solemn assemblies. Your new moons and your appointed feasts, my soul hates. They have become a burden to me. I am weary of bearing them. When you spread forth your hands I will hide my eyes from you. Even though you will make many prayers I will not listen. Your hands are full of blood. Wash yourselves, make yourselves clean. Remove the evil of your doings from before my eyes. Cease to do evil, learn to do good, seek justice, correct oppression, defend the fatherless, plead for the widows'.

The Prophet Isaiah knew the truth and he told the people all his life.

Here is another teaching of his, Isaiah 1 verse 27, 'Zion shall be redeemed by justice and those in her who repent by righteousness'.

You only get redeemed by repenting of the wrongs you've done, turning away from doing wrong and by doing what is right, according to the Ten Commandments, the laws of love'.

How to live righteous lives and not by killing animals or birds. Nor by burnt incense or any other way. These foolish ways are the ways of men. God never gave them to man, only man invented them.

Isaiah also says these words of truth in Chapter 3 verse 12, 'oh my people, your leaders mislead you and confuse the course of your path'.

The leaders are the priests the Pharisees and the Sadducees. These ran the political scene as well as the spiritual scene. They had the power to elect a King or sack one. They had total say in all things. They could put a Prophet on trial and according to Deuteronomy chapter 17 verse 12, 'the man who acts presumptuously by not obeying the priest who stands ministering there to the Lord your God or the Judge, **that** man shall die'.

10

Man was completely at the mercy of these priests, so if these priests told the people that God needed the blood and flesh of burnt offerings what could they do?

If they went against the priests they'd be put to death.

Prophets risked their lives everyday by preaching the truth and sometimes had to go into hiding to stay alive.

Eventually the Prophets were killed, called mad men and heretics by the ruling corrupt priesthood just to keep themselves in luxury and rule over everybody, to please their own egotistical natures.

Jeremiah also spoke out against sacrifices.

Jeremiah chapter 6 verse 20, 'to what purpose cometh there to me incense from Sheba, and the sweet cane from a far country? Your burnt offerings *are* not acceptable, nor your sacrifices sweet unto me'.

God is still telling the people through the Prophets the uselessness of them burning incense and making sacrifices and is asking the reason for them.

It is from the Bible that man has learned cruelty, raping, and murder; for the belief of a cruel God makes a cruel man.

Thomas Paine

God goes on telling the people through Jeremiah Chapter 7 verse 21 to 24, 'thus saith the Lord of hosts, the God of Israel; put your burnt offerings unto your sacrifices, and eat flesh. For I spake not unto your fathers, nor commanded them in the day that I brought them out of the land of Egypt, concerning burnt offerings or sacrifices. But this thing commanded I them, saying, obey my voice, and I will be your God, and ye shall be my people, and walk ye in all the ways that I have commanded you, that it may be well unto you. But they hearkened not, nor inclined their ear, but walked in the counsels *and* in the imagination of their evil heart, and went backward, and not forward'.

God once again saying that he did not give any laws of sacrifices to the people or anything about burning incense. These are the fantasies of priests.

Go back to Isaiah chapter 66 verse 2 to 4, 'but this is the man to whom I will look. He that is humble and contrite in spirit and trembles at my word. He who slaughters an ox is like he who kills a man. He who sacrifices a lamb, like he who breaks a dog's neck. He who presents an oblation offering, like he who offers swine's blood. He who makes a memorial offering of frankincense, like he that blesses an idol. They have chosen their own ways and their soul delights in their abominations. I also will choose affliction for them, and bring their fears upon them. Because when I called, no one answered. When I spoke, they did not listen but they did what was evil in my eyes and chose that in which I did not delight'.

Confirmation again that when he gave the Ten Commandments to Moses he added no more.

11

But the priests don't follow God, they follow their own teachings and then force the people under the threat of death to obey them.

God is omnipresent and is in our life, the animal as well as the human and if you kill an animal then God looks upon that act just as equally as if you killed a man. If you offer an oblation offering, it's as if you're offering swine's blood to God.

Jews do not eat pig's meat as they view it as unclean. Neither will they eat the blood as that is viewed as evil, as they claim the life, the spirit, is in the blood. Now it can be seen how unholy an offering of pig's blood would appear to a Jew, and God is just as much disgusted by these offerings to him.

Can you imagine someone cutting off your finger and offering it to you to eat and expect you to bless him for doing it?

God is omnipresent, is in all life and to offer sacrifices to him is like cutting off parts of him and offering them to him and expecting him to bow to your sins.

It's stupid. How can you expect evil acts to wipe out your sins?

You commit more sins by doing these things.

Nothing will benefit human health and increase the chances for survival of life on Earth as much as the evolution to a vegetarian diet.

Albert Einstein

In the Garden of Eden story, we find in Genesis chapter 1 verse 29, 'behold I have given you every plant yielding seed which is upon the face of all the earth, and every tree will season its fruit. You shall have them for food'.

In the King James version of the Bible it states, 'and for you it shall be as meat'.

So, there you have it, man was made a vegetarian and killing any animal, any living thing is wrong. Thou shalt not kill.

That law applies to all life and not just humans, as God is omnipresent and is in all life and not just humans.

How plain can this be?

And priests are supposed to know the laws of God and teach the people how to live, but it can be seen that they insult God and man alike.

We find God asking the Jews through Isaiah chapter 50 verse 2, 'is my hand shortened that it cannot redeem or do I have no powers to deliver'?

Didn't God make all life and create all the worlds yet these simple fools think there is more power in the blood of animals to wash away sin and is in the all-powerful God who made the blood also.

Can God just not forgive people their wrongs when they're truly sorry and change their ways through his grace, his mercy, rather than the senseless slaughter of animals and burning their flesh and sprinkling their blood?

Of course, he can, and does. He never gave these evil laws of sacrifice to men. They are the invention of the priesthood.

In Hosea, we find another proof of God's grace.

Hosea chapter 13 verse 4, 'I am the Lord your God from the land of Egypt and thou shalt know no God but me, and besides me, there is no saviour'.

The only saviour of mankind, the only one who can forgive sins is God. God alone saves, and not the blood of any animal nor of any man.

St. Paul writes in Hebrews chapter 10 verse 46, 'for it is impossible that the blood of bulls and goats should take away sin'. Consequently, when Christ came into the world he said, 'sacrifices and offering thou has not desired. Also in burnt offerings and sin offerings thou hast taken no pleasure'.

Now if Jesus is also quoting the prophets of the Old Testament and says that sacrifices are wrong, why do the scribes Pharisees and Sadducees not believe him, and why has the Catholic Church followed the priesthood of the Old Testament and not followed Jesus's teachings?

Why does the Catholic Church proclaim that Jesus died on the cross for the sins of the world and that his blood will wash away everyone's sins?

Why does the Catholic Church claim that Jesus' death on the cross has replaced the sacrifice of the Old Testament when the prophets, King David, King Solomon, the wisest man in the Old Testament as well as God and Jesus have said that they are lies.

God did not give these things to the people, he gave the Ten Commandments and 'he added no more'.

People have been brainwashed by the priesthoods of the Old Testament through fear of death if they disobeyed them. The Catholic Church has also picked up this banner of falsehood and put the people under the same threats. They have killed, tortured and burnt people for being heretics and all in the name of Jesus to further the Kingdom of God on earth.

What lies!

What they did was for their own greed and self-aggrandisement to have power over others and live in luxury and everyone to be their slaves.

The Catholic Church is an abomination to God and to mankind. It's time to break free of the shackles of lies and superstitions of the Catholic Church and every other false religion.

Didn't God say 'you should have no other God than me'?

The Catholic Church as did the Pharisees, have made wealth and power over others their first God and broken the first commandment 'thou shalt not kill'.

Millions have died in the name of religion.

'Thou shalt not steal'.

They've stolen from friend and foe alike.

'You shall make no craven images'.

There are idols in every church of Jesus, Mary, Joseph and the Apostles.

'You shall not covet'.

They coveted people's wealth, land, property and have power over others.

'You shall not lie'.

They couldn't speak the truth to save their lives.

13

'Honour the Sabbath day and keep it holy'.

They changed this from Saturday to Sunday at the Council of Nicæa in 365 AD.

'You shall not take God's name in vain'.

They mock God's name every time they speak their lying scriptures. Even their priestly robes are a lie.

'You shall not commit adultery'.

They've lusted after people's wives, husbands, yes even children.

They've exchanged pardon for sins, for money.

How can these corrupt people claim to be the mouthpiece of God on earth when they have broken every law of the Ten Commandments and don't follow them?

How can you put your trust and hope in these liars thinking that they know the way to heaven and that if you stay in their good books they'll get you there also?

These priests are not going to heaven, so how can you hope to get there too?

All you need to do is discriminate. Use the Ten Commandments as your guide and reject everything that goes against them, especially the lies of the priesthood.

How will you get to heaven then, you ask?

Luke chapter 10 verse 25 to 37, 'and behold a lawyer stood up to him to test him saying 'teacher what shall I do to inherit eternal life'?

He said to him, 'what is written in the law, how do you read'? And he answered him, 'you shall love the Lord your God with your heart, with all your soul, with all your strength, with all your mind and you shall love your neighbour as yourself', and he said, 'you have answered right. Do this and you shall live'. But he, desiring to justify himself said to Jesus, 'and who is my neighbour'? Jesus replied 'a man was going down from Jerusalem to Jericho and he fell among robbers who stripped him, beat him and departed leaving him half dead.

Now by chance, a priest was going down that road and when he saw him he passed by on the other side. So likewise, a Levite when he came to the place saw him pass by on the other side. But a Samaritan, as he journeyed came to where he was and when he saw him he had compassion, and went to him and bound up his wounds, pouring on oil and wine. Then he set him on his own beast and brought him to an inn and took care of him, and the next day he took out two denarii and gave them to the inn keeper saying take care of him and whatever more you need I will repay you when I come back'.

Which of these three do you think proved neighbourly to the man who fell among the robbers'?

He said 'the one who showed mercy on him', and Jesus said to him 'go and do likewise'.

Note very carefully that Jesus never once said to the lawyer, 'you know the law, how many sheep, goats and bulls you need to sacrifice to get to heaven and have eternal life'.

He never said so. Nor did the lawyer ask how many he needed to kill to get eternal life?

Jesus asked what the law said and the lawyer replied, 'truly'.

Nor did Jesus claim that he was going to die upon the cross to wash away anybody's sins with his blood. No, not once was blood or sacrifices brought up in the conversation.

'You know the law and what does it say'? said Jesus. The answer was, 'love the Lord your God with all your being and love your neighbour as yourself'.

Love is the one way to get eternal life and get to heaven. No more reincarnating in the flesh and pretending to cleanse the soul.

The Ten Commandments are an explanation of that love.

That is, if you are full of love you won't break any of these laws, you won't harm anyone in thought or your deeds. That is the law and Jesus said that he came to fulfil the law. The law is fulfilled by demonstrating love and didn't Jesus do just that?

He wronged no one. He did not break any of the Ten Commandments, apart from heal upon the Sabbath day but God works on Sabbath days also, and it's not wrong to do good on that day. He loved God with all his being and loved his neighbour as himself. He fulfilled the law of love by demonstrating that love, by healing the sick, and teaching the people how to live their lives which greatly offended scribes, lawyers, Pharisees and Sadducees alike.

Jesus wasn't the only one who offended the ruling class.

The Prophets also offended them by telling them the same truths as Jesus. They taught that sacrifices were wrong and evil. They pleaded for purity in life and obedience to the Ten Commandments. The ruling class put them to death because the people believed them. The rulers were losing their power of control over the people as the people realised the futility of sacrifices and of the priesthood and all they had to do was obey the Ten Commandments, live in love and peace with everybody.

We have a similar story in Luke chapter 18 verses 18 to 24, 'and a ruler asked him, 'good teacher what shall I do to inherit eternal life'?

Jesus said to him, 'why do you call me good? No one is good but God. You know the commandments. Do not commit adultery. Do not kill. Do not steal. Do not bear false witness. Honour your father and mother'.

And he said, 'all these things I have observed from my youth'.

And Jesus said to him, 'one thing you still lack, sell all that you have, distribute it to the poor and you will have treasure in heaven and come follow me'.

But when he heard this he became sad for he was very rich. Jesus looked at him and said how hard it is for those who have riches to enter the Kingdom of God, for it is easier for a camel to go through the eye of a needle than for a rich man to enter the kingdom of God'.

Once again, confirmation that sacrifices are not needed. They are not even mentioned, only to obey the Ten Commandments. The rich man wouldn't get eternal life, that is, reach the plains of the soul because his heart was fixed on earths riches. Fine clothes, big mansion, vineyards etc. These earth riches are the anchor of the soul. When you dispose of them you no longer have any worries or desires holding you down to earth and further incarnations.

I'd be very surprised if you find a priest in heaven as their hearts are full of earth's treasures, fame, lording it over others, obtaining more riches by relieving you of yours with their lies and hypocrisy.

I don't think people realise how the establishment became established. They simply stole land and property from the poor, surrounded themselves with weak minded sycophants for protection, gave themselves titles and have wielded power ever since.

Tony Benn

We have another similar story in Mark chapter 12 verse 28 to 34, 'and one of the scribes came up and heard them disputing with one another, and seeing that he answered well, asked him which commandment is the first of all'? Jesus answered, 'the first is, hear O Israel the Lord our God, the Lord is one. I shall love the Lord your God with all your heart, with all your soul, with all your mind, with all your strength'.

'The second is this, you shall love your neighbour as yourself. There is no other commandment greater than these', and the scribe said to him, 'you are right teacher, you have truly said that He is one and there is no other but He, and to love Him with all your heart, with all your understanding and with all your strength and to love one's neighbour as oneself, is much more than all those burnt offerings and sacrifices', and when Jesus saw that he answered wisely he said to him, 'you are not far from the Kingdom of heaven'.

At last we have a scribe who knows that all God requires is to love Him and one's neighbour as oneself, and that these things are far better than the slaughtering of innocent animals.

As Ecclesiastes states in chapter 5 verse 1, 'guard your steps when you go to the house of God. To draw near to listen is better than to offer the sacrifices of fools for they do not know that what they are doing is evil'.

Isaiah 3 verse 12, 'oh my people, your leaders mislead you and confuse the course of your path'.

The blind leading the blind, the ignorant, evil priesthood confusing the people with their lies.

And Jesus says in Matthew chapter 9 verse 13, 'go and learn what this means, I desire mercy first and not sacrifices, for I came not to call the righteous, but sinners'.

What does it mean?

It means that God desires mercy first, and what is mercy but an act of love, and love fulfils the law. God wants people to love him and all life because He is omnipresent and is **in** our life.

God is not when you kill anything. When you harm any living thing, you do wrong. You do violence to God. He does not want you sacrificing anything. It is evil to do so. When you do a wrong to anything or anyone you do a wrong to God and to yourself, and this debt that you have incurred must be paid for by contrition, true sorrow for doing the wrong, by acts of love to the one you've wronged.

The righteous have no need to repent as they are doing no wrong. Jesus came to teach the sinners, those who do not know the way, to teach them the truths about God, man and the uselessness of sacrifices and priests. Not only were the Pharisees doing and preaching evil but the Catholic Church, by claiming that Jesus takes away the sins of the world by his blood.

That's wrong. The only thing that can take away sin is love. Acts of love, and the only one who can overcome the evil is the one who is doing it by having a change of heart and has stopped doing evil, and do good.

The man who regards his own life and that of his fellow creatures as meaningless is not merely unfortunate but almost disqualified for life.

Albert Einstein

CHAPTER 2

PURGATORY
(The continuation of the transcript of the first CD)

Did you know how the Catholic Church also preaches purgatory?
Purgatory is a place where souls who are not fit for heaven go to, to pay their debts, to suffer purification, to mend their ways and become fit for heaven. Now we have two doctrines which contradict each other. One that Jesus died upon the cross for **everybody's** sins and that his sacrifice has taken the place of the Old Testament sacrifices, and two, that man suffers in purgatory to atone for his sins until he is truly sorry and is fit for heaven.
Now, how silly is this? What applies to the Old Testament also applies to the Catholic Church.
Isaiah 3 verse 12, 'oh my people, your leaders mislead you and confuse the course of your path'.
Jesus often told the Pharisees that they were inconsistent, always changing their teachings and their meanings to suit themselves and here we have the same with the Catholic Church.
They can't lie to God nor to anyone who knows what is true and is fearless of the priesthood. They can threaten you with purgatory, excommunications, the fires of everlasting hell but it does not make them true or real.
So, who do you follow, God's teachings or the priests who dress up and call themselves servants of God?
In First Corinthians chapter 14 verse 20, Paul says 'brethren do not be children in your thinking, be babes in evil but in thinking be mature'.
And in Proverbs chapter 4 verse 5 to 9, Solomon says 'get wisdom, get understanding; do not forsake wisdom, and she will protect you; love her and she will watch over you. For the beginning of wisdom is this. Get wisdom though it will cost all you have, get understanding. Cherish her and she will exalt you; embrace her and she will honour you. She will give you a garland to grace your head and present you with a glorious crown'.
In Ecclesiastes chapter 2 verse 26, Solomon says, 'For *God* giveth to a man that *is* good in his sight wisdom, and knowledge, and joy: but to the sinner he giveth travail, to gather and to heap up, that he may give to *him that is* good before God. This also *is* vanity and vexation of spirit'.
The Bible does have some truths in it as well as lies. You have to discriminate and sort out the wheat from the chaff. Be mature and use your intelligence and discriminate.
Get wisdom, use your reasoning powers, use logic and don't be afraid to think for yourself.
The priests, the Pharisees, the Catholic Church confuse your path. You don't know which is right or wrong but your heart knows, and you go against it every

18

day and follow the priests and think it's ok, because God is guiding the priests and that they have all the answers.

They don't. They are just as lost and as confused as you are, afraid to question the Bible writers who corrupted it in the first place, just so they can rule over people and tell them not to use their brains because only **they** are qualified to interpret the Bible.

How can these people tell you, you know nothing and that you're not qualified to use your own God given brain and hearts where God dwells?

Be mature in your thinking, get knowledge, get wisdom and use logic and your own intelligence and sift through the words, weigh them up, analyse them, test them, get insight into what they mean.

All national institutions of churches, whether Jewish, Christian, or Turkish, appear to me no other than human inventions set up to terrify and enslave mankind, and monopolise power and profit.

Thomas Paine

Paul says in Philippians chapter 1 verse 9, 'and it is my prayer that your love may abound more and more with knowledge and all discernment'.

Paul, reaffirming what has just been said, and the wise ones of the Bible, to get knowledge and all discernment. It's time to use the brain God gave you and not allow yourself to be dictated to by any priest or church, with their fanciful ideas about God or heaven or how they get there. You've already been told obey the Ten Commandments, love God and love your neighbour as yourself. Don't build up treasures on earth and anchor your soul here. Let them go and soar to the spiritual heights. Don't be like the rich man and be miserable. Don't be attached to anything or anyone but God, and you'll get to your heaven.

The priests won't be getting to heaven either. Only those who live the life and not the hypocrites who preach it but don't live it. They are fooling you and themselves.

In Ephesians chapter 2 verse 5, 'by grace you have been saved'.

Yes, by grace, the love of God and not by blood. Not Jesus nor anyone else's nor by animals, but by God's grace. God's love alone'.

Isaiah 50 verse 2, 'is my hand shortened that it cannot redeem or have I no power to deliver'? asks God.

That is insight and that is wisdom.

Did I work out these things all by myself? Am I cleverer than you? Here is the answer.

Jeremiah chapter 33 verse 3, 'call to me and I will answer you and I will tell you great and hidden things which you have not known'.

And Ecclesiastes chapter 2 verse 26, 'for to the man who pleases him, God gives wisdom and knowledge and joy'.

And in Job chapter 32 verse 8 we read, 'the spirit of God in man makes him understand'.

19

There you have the answer.

God's wisdom and his guidance is in my mind and in my heart and in my understanding. God is the wisdom of the wise. God does all the good through man but man in his evil snatches this away, in his ignorance, and claims it was he who did the work or spoke the words.

Jesus gave all the credit to God, 'the Father is in me, he doth the works. The Father has revealed himself through me. Those who have seen me have seen the Father for the Father has revealed himself through the Son'.

True humility and very true.

God does all the work but egotistical arrogant man claims **he** did it. God gives the thought, moves the feelings into loving service and moves your body into doing the work, just as Jesus states. But evil man wants the credit for it. 'Didn't I do well? I saved him, I said this, I did that.

Foolish man will learn different once he gets insight, gets knowledge, gets wisdom, then he will know.

Didn't Jesus say to the rich man, 'why do you call me good? No one is good but God alone'.

So, all the good that people saw Jesus do was actually God working through him and he can do the same through you also, to a greater or lesser extent, depending if you're loving him or earthly treasures.

Jesus is not the only Son of God, as we are all children of God.

The only begotten of the Father God is Christ but Christ is not a man but **universal love** and is omnipresent.

This universal love, Christ is in all life and in man's heart as the still small voice, man's conscience.

When man has purified his heart of all evil thoughts and desires and is pure in thought, word and deed, and loves God with all his being, and his neighbour as himself, and has one desire, to be with God then the Christ within the heart takes full possession of the soul and Christ and man become one.

Just like Jesus demonstrates the love of God. Jesus said he wasn't good only God.

Therefore, it can be seen that Jesus is man but that Christ, spoke through Jesus and did all the miracles. We can be, and will become like Jesus, perfected sons of God, when we purify our hearts, souls and minds by love and righteousness and loving service to others. We can only serve God by serving man and since God is omnipresent we serve God in man and in other life forms. Animals, birds, insects, including plants.

In the ancient world, these things were known but demon priest's, bishops and Popes corrupted this knowledge and forced their creeds upon the world with death threats, hell fires, damnation, excommunication and other lies. They killed millions who stood in their way of world domination. The priesthood, the elite living in luxury while we, like cattle fodder as their slaves.

Mark chapter 7 verses 6 to 9, 'these people honour me with their lips, but their hearts are far from me. In vain do they worship me, teaching for doctrines the commandments of men. You leave the Commandments of God and you hold fast to your traditions', and then he said to them, 'you have a fine way of rejecting the commandments of God in order to keep your traditions'.

So says Jesus.

The priests rejecting the Ten Commandments and forming their own set of beliefs, creeds and traditions and commands for men to follow.

A creed is a set of religious beliefs.

I believe, a fantasy, no proof, like, I believe the moon is made of white cheese. Stupid I know but there is a belief. A fantasy with no real proof, no evidence. Yet man has been to the moon and can disprove that belief.

Likewise, I can disprove the fantasies of the Bible, **with** the Bible and common sense.

Tradition, that is, a habit. It could be smoking, and so a person could smoke fifty cigarettes a day, religiously. This habit has been so repeated that now it has become one of his traditions. He ignores the laws of health and promotes his own tradition.

Likewise, the priesthood has ignored the laws of God and replaced them with their traditions, their beliefs, their creeds and fantasies.

Of what good does it do a man to kneel down on one knee and make the sign of the cross before moving into an aisle and taking a seat?

What benefit is derived from this? What benefit is it to anyone when a man swings a metal ball on a chain and incense is coming out of it?

Twice earlier it's been stated, that God abhors incense, yet they still use it. Why don't they listen to God and not to their own traditions and fantasies?

What benefit does it do anyone to dip their finger in holy water and make the sign of the cross?

What benefits are gained from paraphrasing the words of a service book?

A tape recorder could do the same.

'Behold these people honour me with their lips but their hearts are far away from me'.

You paraphrase sayings in a book but your heart is thinking, 'did I lock the door'? 'What will I get at the shops for tea'? 'I hope my mate turns up so we can go fishing'?

These paraphrasing words, creeds, dogmas are vain and useless and God isn't listening to you, so you're wasting your time and you're not going to heaven, and neither are the priests who invented these things. They are wasting their time also.

You need to have the laws of God in your heart and soul and mind and **live** them and not just paraphrase the fantasies of priests. Stop giving them a tenth of your wages, you can't buy a place in heaven nor God's grace. You can only earn it by living the life with your heart. Feeling love for God and your neighbour. You don't fool God, and neither do priests, no matter how much they try to fantasise or quote corrupt scriptures.

21

Creeds, dogmas, doctrines, rituals, ceremonies, stained glass, altars, mitres, cope -- what have these to do with religion? Religion is in the spirit, the spirit that belongs to all Creation, which expresses itself in every rhythm and manifestation of life, that is revealed in every aspect of nature and in the striving of all idealists and reformers who wish to serve. What has that to do with creeds?

Silver Birch

CHAPTER 3

LIES
(The continuation of the transcript of the first CD)

Of all the tyrannies that affect mankind, tyranny in religion is the worst; every other species of tyranny is limited to the world we live in; but this attempts to stride beyond the grave, and seeks to pursue us into eternity.

Thomas Paine

There are lies in the Bible. How do I know? The Bible tells me so.
Jeremiah chapter 8 verse 8, 'how can you say we are wise and the law of the Lord is with us but behold the lying pen of the scribes has handled it falsely'?
More confirmation, Isaiah 3 verse 12, 'oh my people, your leaders mislead you and confuse the course of your path'.
The scribes are paid by the Pharisees and Sadducees to write their lies and are part and parcel of the corrupt system. The Prophets fought against them, so did John the Baptist, so did Jesus.
They were all put to death.
Until the nineteenth century the Catholic Church carried on the tradition of killing men of truth, forcing others at the point of death, excommunication, hells fires, to get your money and land, and own you mentally and emotionally, just to keep themselves in luxury and rule the world.
The lying pen wasn't just used in the Old Testament it was used to corrupt the books of the New Testament also, and one of the biggest lies of all was the changing of the words about Jesus, God and Peter.
In the Aquarian Gospel of Jesus, the Christ by Levi, (the only true account of Jesus's life), in chapter 128 verses 36 to 38, after Peter said to Jesus, 'you are the Christ, the love of God made manifest in men'. Jesus said, 'behold I give to you the keys to open up the doors of safety for the sons of men, the Holy breath will come upon you and the ten. and in Jerusalem you shall come before the nations of the earth and there proclaim the covenant of God with men, and you shall speak the words of Holy breath, and whatsoever God requires of men as earnest of their faith you shall make known'.
But in Matthew chapter 16 verse 9, we find the work of the lying pen which proclaims, 'I give you the keys of the kingdom of heaven and whatever you find on earth shall be found in heaven and whatever you loosen on earth shall be loosened in heaven'.
This lie, written by the Pope's men and put into the mouth of Jesus gives them a licence to say and do as they wish.
In the middle ages the Pope declared the earth was the centre of creation and that the sun and all the planets revolved around the earth. They called people heretics, imprisoned and tortured them, who went against this doctrine. Now

if the Pope has power from God to fix things on earth and whatever he says God will do in heaven, tell me why God never fixed the earth as the centre of creation and made the sun and all planets revolve around it.

Neither God nor Jesus made Peter a Pope and nor can anyone take Peter's place, but the fantasy goes on and people think the Pope is God's mouthpiece on earth and his followers do whatever he says no matter how evil his wishes are, as though they were the wishes of God.

Another equally big lie is written in Paul's letter, the second letter, Timothy verse 3 to 16, 'all scriptures are God inspired'.

How can all scriptures be inspired by God when they keep contradicting each other?

Is God a moron and getting too old to remember what he said from one minute to another or is it the pen of corrupt priests who alone are qualified to interpret scriptures because they are the ones who wrote them?

Hosea chapter 6 verse 6, 'for I desire steadfast love and not sacrifices. The knowledge of God, rather than burnt offerings'.

Also, Hosea chapter 8 verse 12 to 13, 'though I wrote for him ten thousand precepts of My law, they are regarded as a strange thing. They love sacrifices, they sacrifice flesh and eat it but the Lord has no delight in them'.

More proof from the Prophet Hosea that God does not want sacrifices, but for people to have love for everyone as well as God and have knowledge.

Knowledge of his laws of love, the Ten Commandments.

But the priests don't want the law nor wish to understand it as they love killing. Shedding blood and even the burnt flesh. They ignore everything that God commands them. No matter how many Prophets he sends they kill them, so they can go on with their blood lusting.

Isaiah 66 verse 2 to 4, 'but this is the man to whom I will look. He that is humble and contrite in spirit, and trembles at my word, he who slews as an Ox is like him who kills a man'.

Where is the humility in priests? Where is the trembling at God's laws? Why aren't they living the laws of love? Living the laws of love also means non-violence because love does not inflict pain or suffering on anyone. Nor covet land or treasures, fame and glory as does the priests, Popes and bishops.

Today we have laws of the land to protect us from extortion but the Catholic Church keeps on extorting money from its flock every week and keeps them in slavery to them. Even though slavery was abolished years ago, their heart, soul and mind are still in slavery to the Catholic, Pope's, bishops and priests.

You don't have to be a slave any longer you can break your chains. You can if you use your will power and a little bit of common sense and be free of them.

I say that those who choose a life of conflict; choose to threaten others, choose to allow hunger and poverty and homelessness in your world, which has resources for everybody, those people are the minority. But they are a powerful minority. Very powerful, but there will be a time when the power of good, the power of unseen forces, unheard of forces will penetrate the gloom and fog of your world.

That is why I suggest that many will weep with joy. They will fall to their knees, not in worship with false idolatry, not with false homage, but with weakness before a powerful energy exuding extreme amounts of love, compassion and peace.

Fine Feather

In Micah chapter 6 verse 6 to 8, 'with what shall I come before the Lord and bow myself before God on high? Shall I come before him with burnt offerings, with calves a year old? Will the Lord be pleased with thousands of rams, with myriad streams of oil? Shall I give my first born for my transgressions? The fruit of my body for the sins of my soul'?

'You have been told, O mortal, what is good, and what the Lord requires of you, only to do justice and to love goodness, and to walk humbly with your God'.

Another Prophet is talking about the uselessness of sacrifices. God only requires you to follow the Ten Commandments which are acts of love, to do justice, obey the law, walk humbly with your God, live in love, in kindness, which is a demonstration of love.

Any act of unkindness is breaking the law of love.

Jeremiah chapter 25 verse 3, 'for 23 years from the thirteenth year of Joshua, the son of Amon, King of Judah to this day, the word of the Lord has come to me and I have spoken persistently to you but you have not listened'.

That passage sums up the Pharisees, the Sadducees, the scribes, lawyers and Doctors of the law. It also sums up the Popes, bishops and priests of the Catholic Church.

The Prophets of the Old Testament kept repeating God's message over and over and over. The priesthood has not listened to the words of God or obeyed the Ten Commandments, but their own vain doctrines, dogma's, traditions and fantasies and put to death the Prophets for speaking against them.

John the Baptist came, Elijah reincarnated and he spoke the message of old, told by the Prophets and Jesus also came and told the same things over and over.

Love God with all your being. Love your neighbour as yourself. Sacrifices are not needed or wanted. Just a broken contrite heart and turning away from evil, and obey the law, the Ten Commandments. They also were put to death.

If Jesus were to be born into modern society today he'd say the same thing today and the Catholic Church would proclaim that he is a heretic and seek to take his life once more.

I am repeating what the Prophets and what John the Baptist, as well as Jesus said. You have the quotes from the Bible which you can check.

Will the Catholic Church, the Popes and bishops and priests claim that I am a heretic and seek to take my life also?

How can I be a heretic when I am quoting from the same book they preach from which anyone can read and analyse with God's help.

Also, read what Jesus says in Matthew chapter 23 verse 9, 'call no man Father on earth, for you have one Father who is in heaven'.

Once again, the Catholic Church disobeys Jesus, call no man Father, yet they call themselves Father Paul, Father George, Father Peter etc. They disobey the Prophets, the Ten Commandments and Jesus, yet they proclaim they are God and Jesus's servants. Their mouthpiece on earth.

How much hypocrisy can you stand? When are you going to open your eyes, and see the hypocrisy of the church, the Popes, the bishops and the priests?

Jeremiah chapter 8 verse 8, 'oh my people, your leaders mislead you and confuse the course of your path'.

First Corinthians chapter 14 verse 20, 'brethren do not be children in your thinking. Be babes in evil but in thinking be mature'.

Proverbs 4 verse 5 to 9, 'get wisdom, get insight, do not forsake her and she will keep you. Love her and she will guard you'.

The gain of wisdom is this, 'get wisdom and whatever you get, get insight. Praise her highly and she will exalt you. She will honour you if you embrace her. She will place on your head a fair garland. She will bestow upon you her beautiful Crown'.

I have given you insight into knowledge that is written in your Bible.

Will you be wise?

Will you act upon it or will you forsake it and continue to be slaves to the doctrines, dogmas, creeds traditions and fantasies of the demonic church, her priests, and ignore the laws of God also?

On your judgment day, you cannot cry to God, 'I did not know. I was led to believe the Pope was your voice on earth and I had to obey him and his priesthood'.

God is not fooled, he is all wise, omnipresent. He knows your thoughts words and deeds, even if you've forgotten them.

He hasn't and won't.

You can fool some of the people all the time and all the people some of the time but you cannot fool all the people all the time, you Popes, bishops and priests. God gave you a brain, you use it at work, you use it when you play games, you use it many times a day for many things.

Why don't you use it when it comes to religion? By your own actions and thoughts, you rise or fall. You cannot blame anyone else, so use your own brain. That's why you were given one.

You weren't created to be a mindless robot and do as the priests want you to do. To give them your land, money, your soul, mind and life and live in misery and slavery to them.

Did you know that the Veda's, India's holy books were not just confined to India? That they were also known throughout the world especially in the eastern countries, and that Brahman was their name for God. In Chaldee, Brahman was known. There was a pious Brahman who was called Tara who lived in Ur. His son was so dedicated to the Brahmic faith that he was called A'Bram. A'Bram was later called Abraham and was righteous in the sight of God and became the father of the Arab and Jewish races.

Abraham knew the laws of God, he knew sacrifices were evil and he never sacrificed any birds or animals to God, and God never told him to sacrifice his son Isaac.

That lie was written to give these sacrificial laws more backup, to put the stamp of authority upon them and also claimed that Moses gave the sacrificial laws as well.

Why did Jesus overturn the money changers table, cut the cords that bound the animals and open their cages and set the birds free, if he is the son of God and knows that his father loves blood and eating burnt flesh?

Wouldn't Jesus be going against his father? Wouldn't his father God be offended?

Perhaps the priests would say that he did it because he was taking their place but how could he when he spoke and acted against sacrifices as did the Prophets and they were put to death because they would have lost their wealth and power and control over the people?

CHAPTER 4

ORIGINS OF DECEIT
(The continuation of the transcript of the first CD)

Peace will never be achieved while you are led by vested interests, your churches, your governments, your monarchies. These are not working for world peace.
The existence of your churches, of your religions, is like a fuse, a touch paper igniting the conflict between the people whose only differences are within their minds.

Fine Feather

So, to reiterate, God gave the Ten Commandments and he added no more. All the Prophets and Jesus spoke out against these things. Thou shalt not kill is the law, or one of them. All the Prophets, John the Baptist and Jesus pleaded for purity and life. To love God with all your being and love your neighbour as yourself and do violence to no living thing. They were all put to death for speaking the plain and simple truth.
When did all this deceit begin?
In 270 BC, 70 Jewish emissaries went to the libraries of Alexandria and Egypt where the knowledge of the world was kept, and its history.
It states in the Catholic Bible on page 211 under the heading 'Versions', many versions of the Bible existed in the past. One of these is considered the most important because of its antiquity and its authority. It is known by two names Alexandrian, because it probably was produced in the city of Alexandria and Septuagint so called from the legend that the translation was made by 70 emissaries from Jerusalem about 270 BC.
This version enjoyed great authority at all times. Now, we have a starting point from the Bible, how it was manufactured to suit the politics of the Sadducees. To understand the politics of these people we must examine the Sadducees and the Pharisees in power at that time up to Jesus's life and our present day.

The Pharisees. These people believed in God, life after death, the continuing of the soul and believed that man had a spirit. They believed in punishment for man's sins and that man would get eternal life if he was good. They believed in Angels, messengers from God. They believed in the oral law passed down from mouth to mouth, generation to generation and believed in the written law also.

The Sadducees. They were rich. The aristocrats of the priesthood. They did not believe in Angels. They did not believe in life after death. They did not believe in the continuity of the soul. In fact, they did not believe in the soul or in the spirit. They did not believe in destiny or providence.

They believed a man's wealth was dependent upon himself. They did not believe in the oral law passing down, mouth to mouth. They only believed in the written law which you can see, is what they wrote themselves in 270 BC.

After they obtained copies of documents which they needed for their up and coming book, the libraries of Alexandria were set on fire. At different time periods the Alexandria libraries were set on fire and the finger of blame has always been pointed to the wrong people.

Who would set the libraries of Alexandria on fire and why?

The Sadducees were not priests of God because they did not believe in him, only as a tool to control the people, who did.

But, why become priests?

Because they were the ruling class. They could elect a King or sack one. Expand the boundaries of their country by conquering others or by making them subservient by their Bible, telling them they were God's chosen people and if they weren't nice to them, that their fears and terrible God of war would destroy them and the evidence is in the Bible which they compiled in 270 BC by the 70 emissaries who went to Alexandria to copy various stories from the library there.

The stories they stole were about creation.

The volcano erupting further up the Nile and its after effects re-written as the wrath of God and the ten plagues of Egypt.

The story of the sinking of Atlantis, about 10400 BC, worldwide disasters which were re-written as Noah's Ark and the flood.

The Ark of the Covenant was brought out of Egypt. It was given to Moses by the High Priest of Egypt. God never told the Israelites how to make it. It came from Atlantis and was housed in the great pyramid and had various uses. One, being used in initiation.

I know. I was a trainee priest, who went through initiation and not only saw it but put both my hands upon it and was not struck down dead because we were trained to raise the resistance of our nervous systems to take higher voltages of divine power into our beings, to make us like God men, miracle workers, and control nature, the elements, just as Jesus did years later.

There are many stories in the Bible written by the pen of scribes, paid by the Sadducees. You know about sacrifices being one, now you've heard of some more.

The Sadducees were interested in one thing, to rule and everyone to be their slaves. They used their own people and abused and terrorised them and used laws of sacrifice to make themselves even richer and enslaved the people to them and their deceitful book.

They enjoyed great authority, because they used their wealth and bribed the lawyers, doctors of the law to authenticate the book of lies.

After the sacking of Jerusalem in 70 AD, the Sadducees are said to have magically disappeared.

Yes, but I think they magically reappeared as Christians and corrupted the Catholic Church and turned it into the church of hell just like they did to the Jewish temple.

Jesus said to heal the sick and preach the good news.

Where are the healers and teachers now?

The church of love was murdering millions around the world. Stealing land, valuables, raping, torturing and burning just to rule the world and anyone who joined this motley crew would be exempt from sin because it was all being done for the greater glory of God.

Since when does God sanction the breaking of the Ten Commandments?

He doesn't, but priests claim he does, and all sins are forgiven because they are doing it for God.

The Catholic church is doing it to rule the world. They don't believe in God nor his laws.

Now after 2,000 years of bloody murder, the corrupt church is beyond repair and needs forsaking, as it is pure evil. God is love. Jesus taught love. The Prophets taught love. They taught repentance, and turning away from sin and evil and follow the Ten Commandments.

To love God with all your being and your neighbour as yourself.

Where is the love in the Church today?

The rich think they can buy forgiveness from the priests. They are being lied to. Only the righteous get eternal life, the rest must reincarnate and suffer for all the wrongs they've done.

Isaiah 3 chapter 12, 'oh my people your leaders mislead you and confuse the course of your path'.

Jeremiah chapter 8 verse 8, 'how can you say we are wise and the law of the Lord is with us, but behold the false pen of the scribes has made it into a lie'?

(End of the transcript of the first CD)

CHAPTER 5

THE GLASTONBURY EXCAVATIONS

Science without religion is lame. Religion without science is blind.
Albert Einstein

There are many modern stories that can be told to illustrate the ways in which the priesthood sets out to deny the truth.

One involves two men named Frederick Bligh Bond a highly-respected Architect from Bristol, and John Alleyne who had started to receive automatic writing. They both belonged to the Somerset Archaeological Society with a particular interest in the ruins of Glastonbury Abbey. It had only been partly excavated and they wanted to finish the job.

Alleyne suddenly started receiving automatic writing from three monks who claimed to have lived in the Abbey centuries before. They described the exact layout of the buried chapels which lay under the Abbey ruins, with very specific measurements.

To test the accuracy of the communication the two men approached the Church authorities for permission to excavate the site. Because the Church was aware of the qualifications that Bond had as an Architect, and both men's membership of the Somerset Archaeological Society, permission was given and the dig began.

Both chapels were revealed exactly as stated in the communications, one in 1908 the other in 1919. The Church Authorities were delighted, assuming their success was due to painstaking scholarship and the existence of some hitherto unknown record.

Before the dig began, Alleyne and Bond had given the manuscripts for safe keeping to Sir William Barrett, an honoured professor of the Society of Psychical Research.

He was sworn to secrecy and instructed to open and examine the contents only after the excavations were complete.

All this he did, and was so amazed at the results that he helped Frederick Bligh Bond publish a book, 'The Gates of Remembrance', the story of the psychological experiment which resulted in the discovery of the Edgar Chapel at Glastonbury.

The Churches reaction was shameful.

They treated the two as charlatans and even tried to stop further publication of the book, while church agents attempted to buy up all the copies of the book and destroy them.

Despite strong protests from Sir William Barrett, whose reputation the Church couldn't touch, the county society ostracised both men.

Alleyne died a disillusioned man and Bond exiled himself to America shocked by the vicious reaction from the very people who should have supported him.

31

The Churchmen whose job it was to promote the truth, whatever it may be, in accordance with their Christian principles of honesty and faith, tried to eliminate all traces of the experiment. However, the foundations remain for all to see. The Church authorities could not hide them!

CHAPTER 6

THE CHURCH OF ENGLAND & SPIRITUALISM

The full text of the Majority Report of the Church of England committee appointed by Archbishop Cosmo Lang and Archbishop William Temple to investigate Spiritualism is published below.

This Majority Report was signed by seven of the ten members of the Committee.

The other three signed a Minority Report. The Committee was appointed in 1937.

The Committee appointed in 1937 by the Archbishops to investigate Spiritualism carefully studied the subject for two years and handed in its report. It was expected by the Committee and by the general public that the guidance contained therein would be made available to the rank and file of the Church of England who, up to then, had been given no official lead whatsoever regarding communication with the dead.

When a decent interval had elapsed and no statement had yet been made, enquiries were instituted and it was learned that the House of Bishops had taken the surprising step of pigeon-holing the reports.

For nine years the reports were kept secret, then one morning there mysteriously appeared by post to 'Psychic News' office what purported to be a typed copy of the Majority Report.

The editor got in touch with a member of the Committee he knew was in favour of the report being published, though he was bound by his loyalty to the Church to keep its secrets.

The editor said 'I have a copy of the Majority Report, and I am going to print it, there are one or two phrases that are obscure, because of the careless typing, but I would rather print a slightly inaccurate version than none at all, However, if in the interests of truth you will read what I have and correct it where necessary, then you will be rendering a service to everyone concerned'.

The purported copy was re-typed, a reporter was sent to the member concerned. What the reporter brought back was a carefully corrected type-script, with every comma marked in, missing lines written in the margins, and complete in every detail.

The report was printed in its entirety in 'Psychic News' and with the co-operation of the Press Association extracts from it appeared in newspapers all over the world.

Still the Church preserved a stony silence. Copies of the paper containing the report were sent to all the bishops and the two Archbishops. No comment came except for a protest from the Archbishop of Canterbury.

The editor's printing of the report gave to the rank and file of the Church of England the guidance that had been denied them by the House of Bishops. To Christians all over the world it broke the news that a Committee of influential Churchman, examining Spiritualism on behalf of the Church and at the request of the Archbishops had found that it was true and could be a valuable addition to the Christian ministry.

Below is the full text of the Majority Report submitted to the House of Bishops by the committee of Anglicans appointed by the Archbishops of Canterbury and York to investigate Spiritualism.

THE SIGNATORIES:

Dr. Francis Underhill, Bishop of Bath and Wells; Dr. W. R. Mathews, Dean of St. Pauls;
Canon Harold Anson, Master of the Temple; Canon L. W. Grensted, Nolloth Professor of the Christian Religion at Oxford; Dr. William Brown, Celebrated Harley Street Psychologist;
Mr. P. E. Sandlands, Q.C., Barrister -at-Law; Lady (Gwendolan) Stephenson

In interpreting our evidence it is important to take into account the theories, prevalent among the more experienced and careful Spiritualists, as to the nature and value of the alleged messages delivered through the agency of mediums.
It is pointed out, on the evidence of the "communicators" themselves, that the communicators and guides are themselves at very different levels of spiritual development and of very partial knowledge, and that the "controls" of which they make use may often be very undeveloped personalities who are capable of this particular service because they are closely linked with temporarily disassociated portions of the personalities of the mediums concerned.
There are thus at least three factors which would render messages, especially those of a high order of spiritual or metaphysical value, liable to disturbance, and which lead to the difficulties, generally recognised by spiritualists, which the communicators would in any case find in transmitting messages which do not already lie within the general conditions of our knowledge.
There is, however, nothing inherently contradictory, or necessarily improbable in this account of the conditions involved in such communications. It is, however, no more than a hypothesis, incapable of scientific proof, nor does it assist us in determining the authenticity of the communications themselves.
The verification of these, if it is possible at all, must rest upon ordinary tests.
To say this is not, however, to deny that the communications may sometimes be held to be convincing upon other than scientific grounds.
In any case it seems necessary to distinguish between the sense of contact

34

with departed friends or with 'guides', and the assurance that messages have necessarily any high value because they come through this unusual channel. It is perhaps of some importance to notice that there is general agreement in the communications that time has not the same rigid character as a 'time-series' in the life that lies beyond death.

This is in any case probable on other grounds, but it is of interest as indicating a possible reason why communicators are frequently confused or mistaken as to exact indications of time.

This may not be a failure in their own apprehension of the real significance of events so much as in their power of conveying that apprehension in a form which can be adapted to the mentality of the medium and to the understanding of those to whom the message is directed.

It is often urged as of great significance that Spiritualism in many respects re-affirms the highest convictions of religious people, and that it has brought many to a new assurance of the truth of teaching which had ceased to have any meaning to them.

It is a point of some difficulty, since assurance seems to come along different and even conflicting lines. We cannot ignore the fact that at least one considerable Spiritualist organisation is definitely anti-Christian in character. This divergence of testimony is explained by Spiritualists as due to the continuance of spirits, at least for a period, within the system of beliefs which they have held in this life.

It is held that even though the whole development of the personality is being raised from level to level, the attitudes to truth and goodness taken up in this life persist in the next, and that this somewhat divergent testimony to the truth of Christianity must be explained in this way.

We should add that whatever be the value of this supposed confirmation of the truth of religion, Spiritualism does not seem to have added anything except perhaps a practical emphasis to our understanding of those truths.

Many alleged communications seem, indeed, to fall below the highest Christian standards of understanding and spiritual insight, and indeed below the level of spiritual insight and mental capacity shown by the communicators while still in this life.

While there is insistence upon the supremacy of love comparable with the New Testament assertion that 'God is Love' the accounts sometimes given of the mediatorial work of Christ frequently fall very far below the full teaching of the Christian Gospel, seeming to depend rather upon some power of working a miracle of materialisation (in the Resurrection appearances) than upon a radical and final acceptance of the burden of guilt of man's sin, and a victory wrought for us upon the Cross.

Nevertheless, it is clearly true that the recognition of the nearness of our friends who have died, and of their progress in the spiritual life, and of their continuing concern for us, cannot do otherwise, for those who experience it, than add a new immediacy and richness to their belief in the Communion of

Saints.

There seems to be no reason at all why the Church should regard this vital and personal enrichment of one of her central doctrines with disfavour, so long as it does not distract Christians from their fundamental gladness that they may come, when they will, into the presence of their Lord and Master, Jesus Christ Himself, or weaken their sense that their fellowship is fellowship in Him.

It is claimed by Spiritualists that the character of many events in the Christian revelation, as recorded in the Gospels, is precisely that of psychic phenomena, and that the evidence for the paranormal occurrences which Spiritualism has adduced strongly confirms the historicity of the Gospel records, in the sense that they also are records of paranormal occurrences, including instances for example, of clairvoyance (in the story of Nathaniel) and of materialisation (in the feeding of the five thousand, and above all the narrative of the Resurrection appearances).

The miracles of Healing are acclaimed as closely parallel to the healings performed through mediums. it is strongly urged that if we do not accept the evidence for modern psychic happenings, we should not, apart from long tradition, accept the Gospel records either.

It is certainly true that there are quite clear parallels between the miraculous events recorded in the Gospel and modern phenomena attested by Spiritualists. And if we assert that the latter must be doubted because they have not yet proved capable of scientific statement and verification, we must add that the miracles, and the Resurrection itself, are not capable of such verification either.

We must therefore ask what the proper Christian grounds of belief in these central truths of Christianity are. The answer to this question is clearly that we believe upon a basis of faith, and not of demonstrable scientific knowledge.

Our grounds for this faith are to be found either in a direct mystical assurance that Jesus of Nazareth, as we have received Him, is indeed God's word to us, or, more broadly, in the apprehension of ethical and spiritual values.

We do not accept the Gospel's because they record wonders, but because they ring true to the deepest powers of spiritual apprehension which we possess. But if this is so, we must clearly apply similar criteria to the claims of Spiritualists, and this means that while we regard some part of these claims as matter proper to the scientist, we regard some other parts of these claims as not properly capable of scientific verification or dispute, but at the same time, as deserving the consideration of Christians upon grounds of another kind.

It has been seen, in the account of the evidence submitted to our Committee, that as far as rigid scientific tests are concerned very little if anything remains both verifiable and inexplicable out of the whole mass of paranormal phenomena.

Modern psychological knowledge has revealed a wide range of powers and of possible sources of misunderstanding in our subconscious or unconscious mind. When these are combined with the possibility of thought-transference, of telepathy, many communications delivered through mediums seen capable of explanation.

We have to notice that no good evidence for telepathy itself is yet forthcoming, but probably a majority of scientists would accept it as a fact without pretending to offer an explanation of it. If telepathy is denied, the evidence that these communications do come from discarnate spirits is greatly strengthened on the scientific side.

But the tests applied by scientists as such are in their very nature experimental, objective and impersonal. It is necessary to ask whether such tests do not in themselves invalidate an inquiry into values which are in essence, personal and spiritual.

The experiences which many people have found most convincing are of a kind which could hardly occur in the atmosphere of scientific investigation. They are sporadic, occasional and highly individual. They could not possibly be repeated or submitted to statistical analysis.

It is worthwhile to notice in this connection that in the ordinary affairs and beliefs of human life we do not ask for scientific verification of this kind. We accept many things as certain in the realm of personal relationships upon the basis of direct insight.

When we say that we know our friends, we mean something very different from saying that we can give a scientific and verifiable account of them. But we are nonetheless sure of our knowledge. Similar certainties are to be found in the sphere of mystical experience.

It may well be that in this matter of the evidence of the survival of the human personality after death, we are dependent exactly upon this same kind of insight, and that a scientific verification, though valuable where it can be obtained, is of secondary importance, and only partially relevant.

And this is precisely the situation in which we find ourselves in our assurance of Christianity itself.

'We walk by faith, and not by sight.'

It is thus a weakness, rather than a strength, in the Spiritualist position that it has been represented as resting upon scientific verification. If rigid scientific methods are applied it is probable that verification will never be attained.

We may sum up the position from the point of view of science as follows: There is no satisfactory scientific evidence in favour of any paranormal physical phenomena (materialisations, apports, telekinesis, etc.) All the available scientific evidence is against the occurrence of such phenomena.

Further, the hypothesis of unconscious mental activity in the mind of mediums or sensitive is a strong alternative hypothesis to that of the action of a discarnate entity in cases of mental mediumship.

Thus the strictly scientific verdict on the matter of personal survival can only be one of non-proven. Again the whole question of Extra Sensory Perception is still a matter of scientific subjudice.

On the other hand certain outstanding psychic experiences of individuals, including certain experiences with mediums, make a strong prima facie case for survival and for the possibility of spirit communications while philosophical, ethical and religious considerations may be held to weigh heavily on the same side.

When every possible explanation of these communications has been given, and all doubtful evidence set aside, it is generally agreed that there remains some element as yet unexplained.

We think that it is probable that the hypothesis that they proceed in some cases from discarnate spirits is the true one.

That so much can be said, even in so cautious a form, involves very important consequences, and makes necessary certain warnings.

It is abundantly clear, as Spiritualists themselves admit, that an easy credulity in these matters opens the door to self-deception and to a very great amount of fraud.

We are greatly impressed by the evidence of this which we received, and desire to place on record a most emphatic warning to those who might become interested in Spiritualism from motives of mere curiosity or as a way of escaping from their responsibility of making their own decisions as Christians under the guidance of the Holy Spirit.

It is legitimate for Christians who are scientifically qualified to make these matters a subject of scientific inquiry, though, as we have already said, such inquiry has its necessary limitations.

But it is not legitimate, and it is unquestionably dangerous, to allow an interest in Spiritualism, at a low level of spiritual value, to replace that deeper religion which rests fundamentally upon the right relation of the soul to God Himself.

It is necessary to keep clearly in mind that none of the fundamental Christian obligations or values is in any way changed by our acceptance of the possibility of communication with discarnate spirits.

Where these essential principles are borne in mind, those who have the assurance that they have been in touch with their departed friends may rightly accept the sense of enlargement and of unbroken fellowship which it brings.

It is important to distinguish between assurance of this personal contact and assurance of the accuracy and authority of the messages received. As we have seen, and as many Spiritualists admit, there is every probability that even authentic messages would be liable to distortion.

There is a very great danger of misdirection if such messages are accepted as giving authoritative guidance unless they are checked by our own human reason under guidance of the Holy Spirit received through prayer.

But there is no reason why we should not accept gladly the assurance that we are still in closest contact with those who have been dear to us in this life, who are going forward, as we seek to do ourselves, in the understanding and fulfilment of the purpose of God.

We cannot avoid the impression that a great deal of Spiritualism as organised has its centre in man rather than God, and is, indeed, materialistic in character. To this extent, it is a substitute for religion, and is not in itself religious at all.

We are impressed by the unsatisfactory answers received from practising Spiritualists to such questions as, 'Has your prayer life, your sense of God, been strengthened by your Spiritualistic experiences?'

This explains in great part the hesitancy of many Christians to have anything to do with it.

But if Spiritualism does, in fact, make so strong an appeal to some, it is at least in part because the Church has not proclaimed and practised its faith with sufficient conviction.

There is frequently little real fellowship even between the living, and the full and intimate reality of the Communion of Saints is often a dead letter.

Spiritualism claims, in fact, to be making accessible a reality which the Church has proclaimed but of which it has seemed only to offer a shadow. This is, of course, only a part of the truth.

For many the appeal of Spiritualism rests upon much lower motives. It may stimulate curiosity in the bizarre. It may offer consolation upon terms which are too easy.

It may afford men the opportunity of escaping the challenge of faith which, when truly proclaimed, makes so absolute a claim upon men's lives that they will not face it but turn aside to some easier way.

It is often held that the practice of Spiritualism is dangerous to the mental balance as well as to the spiritual condition, of those who take part in it, and it is clearly true that there are some cases where it has become obsessional in character.

But it is very difficult to judge in these cases whether the uncritical and unwise type of temperament which does show itself in certain Spiritualists is a result or a cause of their addiction to these practices.

Psychologically it is probable that persons in the condition of mental disturbance, or lack of balance, would very naturally use the obvious opportunities afforded by Spiritualism as a means of expressing the repressed emotions which have caused their disorder.

This is true of Christianity itself, which frequently becomes the outlet, not only for cranks, but for persons who are definitely of unstable mentality.

It should be noticed that Spiritualists themselves are very much alive to the danger to those who are already unstable, and even to those who are stable, where the motives are wrong and precautions as to sincerity inadequate.

Whatever else is clear in a matter where the evidence is difficult to interpret, it is certain that Spiritualism has every need of the high standards of

39

Christianity and of its witness to a life which rests by faith upon God, and which is thereby freed from the conflicts of desire and of purpose to which all lives not so grounded are liable.

The view has been held with some degree of Church authority, that psychic phenomena are real but that they proceed from evil spirits. The possibility that spirits of a low order may seek to influence us in this way cannot be excluded as inherently illogical or absurd, but it would be extremely unlikely if there were not also the possibility of contact with good spirits. The belief in Anglican guardians or guides has been very general in Christianity.

But in any case, the Christian life is grounded upon God, and its fundamental activities are prayer and worship, which issue in loving worship of mankind. A life so grounded has nothing to fear from evil influences or powers of any kind.

The Church of England, for reasons of past controversy, has been altogether too cautious in its references to the departed. Anglican prayers for the departed do not satisfy people's needs, because the prayers are so careful in their language that it is not always evident that the departed are being prayed for, as contrasted with the living.

In general we need much more freedom in our recognition of the living unity of the whole Church, in this world and in that which lies beyond death. But detailed suggestions on this point should be matters of dispute, and lie beyond the main purpose of this report.

If Spiritualism, with all aberrations set aside and with every care taken to present it humbly and accurately, contains a truth, it is important to see that truth not as a new religion, but only as filling up certain gaps in our knowledge, so that where we already walked by faith, we may now have some measure of sight as well.

It is, in our opinion, important that representatives of the Church should keep in touch with groups of intelligent persons who believe in Spiritualism. We must leave practical guidance in this matter to the Church itself.

The power that fashioned the universe is not impressed because you build a great cathedral and fill it with beautiful music and have stained glass windows and impressive processions. You cannot imprison the Great Spirit in a building.

Silver Birch

CHAPTER 7

REINCARNATION & OTHER TOPICS
(The transcript of the second CD)

Your churches have failed you; they are bankrupt. Your men of science have failed you; they seek to destroy instead of building. Your philosophers have failed you; theirs is but the empty talk of idle speculation.
Your statesmen have failed you; they have not learned the supreme lesson that only through sacrifice can peace come to your world.

Silver Birch

People think that reincarnation is an Indian belief but this knowledge was worldwide until the year 553 AD where at the second Council of Constantinople, it was outlawed and declared as heresy.

If reincarnation is to be outlawed, then why was it not removed from the Bible altogether?

In Malachi chapter 4 verse 5 'behold, I will send you Elijah the prophet before the coming of the great and dreadful day of the Lord, and he shall turn the heart of the fathers to the children, and the heart of the children to their fathers, lest I come and smite this land with a curse'.

The Prophets spoke about sacrifices; they were not believed.

They spoke of the coming King the Messiah from the House of David.

The Catholic Church believes that one, yet they don't believe that John the Baptist is Elijah reincarnated. They seem very selective in what or whom they believe.

If all scriptures are God inspired, then surely God knows what he is talking about and doing.

This statement is repeated in Matthew chapter 11 verse 9, 'why then did you go out, to see a Prophet? Yes, I tell you and more than a Prophet. This is He of whom it is written. Behold I send my messenger before thy face. Who shall prepare thy way before thee'?

And in verse 14, 'and if you're willing to accept it, he is Elijah who is to come. He who has ears to hear let him hear'.

It is obvious that the Catholic Church does not accept what Jesus says, nor has ears to hear with.

The Prophet stated, as did Jesus, that John the Baptist is Elijah reincarnated yet the Catholic Church says this is heresy. Therefore, they are claiming that their leader, Jesus is a heretic.

In Matthew chapter 17 verse 10 to 13, 'and the disciples asked him, then why do the scribes say that first Elijah must come. He replied, 'Elijah does come and he has to restore all things. But I tell you that Elijah has already come and

41

they did not know him but did to him whatever they pleased. So also, the Son of Man will suffer at their hands'.

Then the disciples understood that he was speaking to them of John the Baptist. Confirmation that Elijah had reincarnated and was John the Baptist again from the mouth of Jesus.

So why do the Catholic priests go against the words of God, his Prophets, Malachi and even call Jesus a liar also?

The Gospel of Mark repeats these words of Jesus in chapter 9 verse 13, 'but I tell you that Elijah has come and they did to him whatever they pleased as it was written of him'.

In Luke chapter 7 verse 24 to 27 we have it again, 'what did you go out into the wilderness to behold? A reed shaken by the wind. What then did you go out to see? A man clothed in soft raiment. Behold those are who gorgeously apparelled and live in luxury are in Kings Courts. What then did you go out to see? A Prophet? Yes, I tell you, and more than a Prophet. This is he of whom it is written. Behold I send my messenger before thy face who shall prepare thy way before thee'.

Once again, the Catholic Church ignores Malachi, and Jesus, that John the Baptist is Elijah reincarnated. How can these bishops have a meeting and declare reincarnation heresy and Gods Prophets and Jesus liars and yet pretend to follow Jesus?

In Jeremiah chapter 25 verse 3, 'for twenty-three years from the thirteenth year of Joshua, the son of Amon King of Judah to this day, the word of the Lord has come to me and I have spoken persistently to you but you have not listened'.

What was true in the days of Jeremiah was and is true of the Catholic Church from its earliest meetings of 250 AD, 553 AD right up to date. They take no notice of God, his Prophets, nor of Jesus or his disciples but follow their own fantasies and traditions, creeds and dogmas, and have you believe that God and Jesus are liars.

In Matthew, we find out more about reincarnation in chapter 16 verse 13 to 14, 'who do men say the son of man is'? And they said, 'some say John the Baptist, other's say Elijah, and others said Jeremiah or one of the Prophets'.

It is stupid for the writers to say John the Baptist, as John and Jesus were of the same age, give or take three months, and John the Baptist was already there. And it's stupid to say he was Elijah as John the Baptist is he. But it goes to show that the belief in reincarnation was worldwide in those days before the Catholic Church.

Abraham was raised in the Vedas; India's holy books and reincarnation was one of the truths they learnt and passed on to his children.

Further proof of reincarnation is found in John chapter 9 verses 1 to 2 "and as he passed by, he saw a man blind from birth, and his disciples asked him Rabi who sinned this man or his parents that he was born blind'?

Now if a man is born blind how could he have sinned unless he had been here before and was paying off debts that he had incurred in a previous incarnation? There are thousands of people around the world who have knowledge of previous incarnations. If reincarnation isn't true, why do so many people claim a past life memory or several past life memories?

God is sending Elijah back to before Messiah's face to pave the way for his coming. Malachi and Jesus reaffirm this in various scriptures.

So, why does a council of bishops proclaim this as heresy in 553 AD in Constantinople?

Are God and the Prophet Malachi as well as Jesus, liars?

Is the Catholic Bishop right in calling them liars? Or is it the church of bishops who are the liars?

The answer is the church and his bishops and I'll tell you why.

Authors note: the following statements about reincarnation and the law of good and bad karma through rebirth as a punishment for deeds done in previous lives do not sit well with a Spiritualists' beliefs.

Reincarnation goes hand in hand with the laws of karma. Jesus taught that a person reaps what he sows. Now if you harm anyone in thought, word or deed, the day will come when you will suffer for what you've done. Moses taught the same law summed up in, 'an eye for an eye, tooth for a tooth, a life for a life.

In the law of karma, we see the justice side of God enacted out in reincarnation. People are born blind, deaf, dumb, deformed in mind, body or spirit because in past incarnations they broke the law of love and harmed others.

God is not a moron who willy nilly inflicts suffering upon people out of pure fancy or boredom. People are not born healthy or unhealthy out of some lottery system. They are born that way because of good or bad karma. It would be unjust of God to allow children who have never been here before to be born deaf, dumb, blind or inflicted in anyway who have done nothing wrong.

The bishops, Popes and priests had to destroy any belief in these two laws of God to stay in power.

If people knew that they suffer for their crimes, if not in this life then certainly in a future incarnation that would make the laws of sacrifice a lie. They would realise that all the sacrificial laws were written by the priesthood and use Moses' name as their scapegoat for all their lies.

It also proves Jesus did not take the place of the sacrifices of the Old Testament and nor did he die for your sins or that his blood washes away your sins either.

It also means that the priesthood is out of a job, especially since they preach the doctrine of purgatory where people suffer to become fit for heaven. If the people know the truth and they can't be hoodwinked by their church anymore, then the priesthood would have to be abandoned and find a proper job, and earn their wages by the sweat of their own brows instead of getting you to keep them out of fear and lies.

Now you know why it was outlawed in 553 AD at the second Council of Constantinople, because it took away their power of enslavement over you. You've been hoodwinked by the priesthood who have dressed up and called themselves priests, bishops and Popes, claiming to be servants of God yet they don't follow the Ten Commandments. They've broken every one and still use incense in the church and ignore what the Prophets and Jesus says.

'Call no man father', hypocrisy everywhere and direct disobedience to God, the Prophets and Jesus, and calling them all liars. Everyone's a liar according to their teachings which are perverted.

If John the Baptist is not Elijah reincarnated, as the Prophet Malachi prophesied, and as Jesus claimed then Jesus cannot be the Christ and he is yet to come because Elijah must go before Messiah's face and prepare his way.

Who are you going to believe, the priesthood or God's messenger Malachi and Jesus himself who said that John is Elijah reincarnated?

CHAPTER 8

PARENTHOOD OF JESUS
(The continuation of the transcript of the second CD)

We come now to the topic of Joseph being the father of Jesus.

According to the compilers of the New Testament Joseph is not the father of Jesus but Lord God Almighty himself.

In the Gospel of Matthew chapter 1 verses 1 to 16 the compilers give a genealogy. 'The book of genealogy of Jesus Christ, the Son of David, the Son of Abraham'.

In this first statement, they are saying that Jesus Christ came from the bloodline of Abraham and David. But after a long line of genealogy it states in verse 16, 'and Jacob the father of Joseph, the husband of Mary, of whom Jesus was born who was called the Christ'.

They say Joseph is from David's line but he is not Jesus' father. If Joseph is not the father of Jesus how can Jesus be from David's blood line?

He cannot be.

Therefore, if Jesus has not got Joseph as his dad then he cannot be the Christ, and he is yet to come. You remember the writers claim that John the Baptist is not Elijah reincarnated? So, Elijah has not yet appeared and neither has the Christ, as he is to come from David's line.

In Isaiah chapter 7 verse 14 we read, 'behold a young woman shall conceive and bear a son and shall call his name Emmanuel'.

A young woman, not a virgin. Not a woman visited by God and made pregnant, but a young woman shall conceive, and how do women conceive? By having sex with a man. With Joseph from David's line.

Now you may argue foolishly, and say that Mary was a virgin. Yes, as all women are until they have sex and conceive and bear children. So, Mary was a virgin who had sex on her wedding night and conceived and bore Jesus, Joseph's son about 9 months later.

Otherwise Jesus is not from David's line and cannot be the Christ.

There are many instances in the four gospels where it is written that Jesus refers to himself as the Son of Man.

It is written 72 times!

Now is Jesus once again to be called a liar?

If he is the Son of Man, then a man must be his father.

Is this not correct?

In First Thessalonians verse 20, Paul tells people to test everything. It is clear that the world has not tested the books of the Bible, otherwise they'd see the lies and contradictions in them and reject them and sort out the wheat from the chaff.

45

In second Timothy, Paul says in verse 8, 'remember Jesus Christ, risen from the dead descended from David as preached in my gospel'.

Paul knew that Jesus came from the blood line of David and that Joseph was his father.

Here is a man who tested everything, analysed and used his intelligence and logical mind to decipher what was true.

The Prophet Jeremiah wrote in chapter 33 verse 15 to 16, 'in those days, at that time I will cause a righteous branch to spring forth for David, and he shall execute justice and righteousness in the land. In those days Judas shall be saved and Jerusalem will dwell securely and this is the name by which it will be called. The Lord is our righteousness'.

Now we have two Prophets claiming that Christ will come from David's line. Are we going to be like the Catholic bishops and call them liars or shall we trust their words?

Romans chapter 1 verse 1 to 3, 'Paul, a servant of Jesus Christ called to be an Apostle, set apart for the gospel of God which he promised beforehand through his Prophets and the Holy Scriptures. The gospel concerning his son who was descended from David according to the flesh'.

Paul stating the plain and truth, that Jesus was a descendant of David according to the flesh and Joseph had sex with Mary who became pregnant, and Jesus was born to them both according to the flesh.

How plain is that?

Paul lived in the days of Jesus, he knew the disciples who also knew Mary and Joseph who were Jesus' parents.

In Luke chapter 2 verse 41 we read, 'now his parents went to Jerusalem every year at the feast of the Passover'.

His parents, Jesus' mother and father Joseph.

Verse 43, 'and when the feast was ended and they were returning, the boy Jesus stayed behind in Jerusalem, his parents did not know this'.

Again, it is written 'his parents', his father and mother.

Verse 48, 'and when they saw him they were astonished and his mother said to him, 'son why have you treated us so? Behold, your father and I have been looking for you anxiously'.

'Your father and I', how plain is that?

Mary stating that Joseph is Jesus' father and Mary obviously knows who had sex with her and got her pregnant. It was Joseph and not God, as the bishops wrote in the Bible.

Joseph made Mary pregnant according to the flesh and Jesus was born from David's line.

John chapter 1 verse 45, 'Philip found Nathaniel and said to him, we have found him of whom Moses wrote about in the law, and about whom the Prophets wrote, Jesus of Nazareth, the son of Joseph'.

John chapter 6 verse 42, they said, 'is not this Jesus the son of Joseph whose father and mother we know? How is it then that he saithe, I came down from heaven'?

Two more accounts from Jesus' disciples who knew Jesus stating that Joseph is his dad.

These foolish claims by the Catholic Church remind me of a story.

A lady watching her son in a passing out parade seeing him out of step with the other soldiers exclaimed, 'look they are all out of step except out Brian'.

These deceitful bishops and Popes who corrupted the Bible and changed it with all their meetings since 215 AD even up to the 18th century, claim that God, Moses, the Prophets, John the Baptist, Jesus and all his disciples are all out of step with reality and they alone are the ones who are right.

Who are you going to believe?

The people who knew Jesus, walked with him, talked with him and knew his parents, or the deceitful, corrupt bishops who ignore the Ten Commandments, make idols, burn incense, claim sacrifices are what God needs and loves, and ignore Jesus saying to call no man father.

But they love to wear that title also and even corrupt the truth and outlaw reincarnation and invite silly dogmas, creeds and traditions at their silly egotistical meetings to keep themselves in power over you.

Did you know that in the 12th century some silly Pope come up with the idea that Mary was divinely created? That Anna, her mother was visited by God and she conceived and bore Mary.

Now this was not made official until 1854 when some other stupid Pope gave it the seal of approval. For 1200 years Mary was being conceived and born the normal way the way of the flesh, and Joachim had sex with Anna and Mary was born. But after that it was proclaimed an immaculate conception, but it was not made official for another 600 years.

And people sang silly fantasy songs and even pray 'immaculate Mary'.

Stupid people will believe anything rather than use their brains because they don't want to upset the deceitful Pope and bishops, in case they get excommunicated and classed as a heretic and are damned to eternity in hell. How silly!

More silly sayings and fantasies from these bishops just to keep you in line.

In Genesis chapter 18 verse 10 we read, 'and he said I will certainly return unto thee according to the time of life and, lo, Sarah thy wife shall have a son'.

In verse 11, 'now Abraham and Sarah were old and well stricken in age and it ceased to be with Sarah after the manner of women'.

She stopped having her periods as she was 90 years old.

In verse 14, 'is there anything too hard for the Lord? At the time, appointed I will return unto thee according to the time of life and Sarah shall bear a son'.

Here we have a story of a flesh and blood men who visit Abraham, he cooks meat for them they eat it and drink. The leader of the men is supposed to be God almighty and he is going to visit Sarah and make her pregnant.

47

In Genesis chapter 25 verse 21, 'and Isaac prayed to the Lord for his wife because she was barren and the Lord granted his prayer and Rebekah his wife conceived'.

Is almighty God the father of the flesh and blood of Isaac, and is he the father of Rebekah's children Jacob and Esau?

Are the fanciful writers trying to say that God is the father of the Jewish race, and that they are divine, and the rightful rulers of earth, but the rest of humanity are not?

Not to be outdone by the Old Testament writers, the New Testament writers claim God had sex with Anna and Mary was immaculately conceived, and then he had sex with his daughter Mary and committed incest and produced Jesus.

You may feel offended or disgusted by this but these things are instigated by the lying pen of the Church who wrote, and claims, these things to be true.

Is the penny starting to drop? Are you not yet convinced you're being lied to?

CHAPTER 9

THE STAR OF BETHLEHEM
(The continuation of the transcript of the second CD)

Great Spirits have always encountered opposition from mediocre minds.
Anyone who becomes seriously involved in the pursuit of science becomes
convinced that there is a spirit manifest in the laws of the universe – a spirit
vastly superior to man.

Albert Einstein

Here is the true story about the so-called Star of Bethlehem.

It is written that three wise men came from the east and that they followed the star. Now if they had followed the star wouldn't it have led them to Bethlehem where Jesus was and not to Jerusalem?

Or perhaps the star lost its way and needed the wise men to guide it.

The wise men, what were they wise about? How come they were called wise? The book does not say.

These had to make enquiries in Jerusalem about the birth of a King. Herod called his wise men and they said that he was to be born in Bethlehem. So, the wise men went off to find him.

Matthew chapter 2 verse 9, 'when they had heard the king they departed and, lo, the star which they had seen in the east went before them till it came to rest over the place where the child was'.

There has been much speculation about this star which did not exist. Some people today claim it was a UFO and there has even been a Christmas song about this UFO story.

More silliness.

The wise men came from beyond Euphrates. The Magi lived in Persia. They were wise because they could read the stars. They were astrologers and they divined that it was time for a master soul to be born and that this soul, his birth place was somewhere in or near to Jerusalem. So, the Magi went in search of this master soul to be born on earth.

There have been many such masters or Christ men before Jesus, which I'll speak about shortly.

The Magi went to Jerusalem and made enquiries about this new born King. Herod got to hear about them, had them brought to Court to see what all the fuss was about. After being told, he called in the priests and asked what the Prophets had to say and was told that it was predicted that such a one will be born in Bethlehem. Herod told the Magi where to look and so they headed off to Bethlehem and made further enquiries there and found what they were looking for.

All without the help of a UFO or a star.

You know your horoscope that is printed in newspapers, based upon your date and time of birth and that there are twelve signs of the zodiac, and it takes one year for our sun to pass through these signs? On the larger scale, it takes our sun about twenty-six thousand years to pass through the signs of the zodiac. It takes about two thousand, one hundred and sixty years for the sun to pass through one of these signs and each sign is called an age.

The sun had already passed through the sign of Aries and had entered Pisces. At the beginning of every age a master soul incarnates to manifest the Christ spirit on earth, to lead the people back upon the paths of righteousness from which they had gone astray. Back to a loving God and treating their neighbours as themselves and doing violence to no living thing.

Now before Jesus and the age of Pisces there lived another Christ man.

In Hebrews chapter 7 verse 1 to 3, 'for this Melchisedec King of Salem, priest of the highest God. He is the first, by translation of his name. King of Righteousness and he is also King of Peace. He is without father or mother or genealogy and has neither the beginning of days nor end of life but resembling the Son of God he continues a priest forever'.

Did you get that?

King of Righteousness. King of Peace, just as Jesus is portrayed. But unlike Jesus it is written that he didn't have a father or mother or ancestry. The lying pen of the Sadducees in the Old Testament were not the only ones who wrote with a lying pen. If a person lives on earth and has a flesh body, then he must have had a flesh blood mother and father. But these writers claim that he alone went against God's laws and creation.

This Melchisedec, King of Righteousness and the King of Peace lived about two thousand years before Jesus and said that he would return. So, we have evidence of a Christ man two thousand years before Jesus.

In Hebrews chapter 7 verse 15 speaks about Jesus. 'This becomes even more evident when another priest arises in the likeliness of Melchisedec,' and in verse 17 'but it is witnessed of him though art a priest forever after the order of Melchisedec'.

So, Jesus was likened unto Melchisedec, King of Righteousness, King of Peace.

As stated earlier, Christ incarnates at the beginning of every age.

You've also had Krishna who lived about three thousand years before Jesus. You've also had Zarathustra and even Enoch was also a Christ man.

We also have the story of Mishra's and his birth etc. was exactly like Jesus. It would look like the story tellers of the Catholic Church re-wrote the story of Jesus and based it upon the story if Mishra's and, also through him, a bit of Melchisedec for more back up.

But was the Mishra's story copied from Mishra's or from an even earlier Christ story belonging to someone else?

We are about to move into the Age of Aquarius and another God man is going to manifest the Christ spirit at the beginning of this age too. When the Bible

50

speaks about the last days, Jesus is not speaking about the end of the world but the last days of Pisces and the beginning of the Age of Aquarius. It is said that God is the same yesterday, today and tomorrow and he never changes.

If that is true he should be doing immaculate conceptions today, shouldn't he? If he isn't doing them today, then he certainly never did them in the past and won't be doing any in the future, and if God gave the Israelites the Promised Land and killed all the enemies and brought about the ten plagues of Egypt, why is he not active today?

If Moses saw God's face to face and not only Moses but seventy Jewish Priests in the desert, then why isn't he showing himself today?

If Abraham and Lot saw him face to face where is he at today?

Did you know God is portrayed as a flesh and blood man in the Old Testament in the Garden of Eden story?

Another fanciful piece of illusion.

In Genesis chapter 33 verse 24 you read, 'and Jacob was left alone and a man wrestled with him until the breaking of the day'.

In chapter 32 verse 28 to 30 he said, 'your name shall no more be called Jacob but Israel, for you have striven with God and with men and have prevailed'. Then Jacob asked him, 'tell me I pray, your name,' but he said, 'why is it that you ask me my name'?

And then he blessed him, so Jacob called the place Peniel saying, 'for I have seen God face to face and yet my life is preserved'.

In Exodus chapter 15 verse 3 it states, 'the Lord is a man of war, the Lord is his name'.

In the next story, we find Abraham speaking to God and we find that Abraham is cleverer than God and much more compassionate.

Genesis chapter 18 verse 23 to 33, 'then Abraham drew near and said, wilt thou indeed destroy the righteous with the wicked? Suppose there are fifty righteous in the city, wilt thou then destroy the place and not spare it for the sake of fifty righteous who are in it? Far be it for me to do such a thing, to slay the righteous with the wicked so that the righteous shall be as the wicked. Far be it from me shall not the Judge of all the earth do right'?

And the Lord said, 'if I find that in Sodom fifty righteous in the city, I will spare the whole place for their sake'.

This exchange goes on until Abraham whittles the numbers down to ten, haggling like a good Jew should and proves he's more compassionate and wiser than God Almighty.

The lying pen of the scribes again paid by the Sadducees to write their lies.

Fancy portraying God who is omnipresent, all wise and all powerful as a weak man who cannot beat a Jew in a wrestling match, nor is as wise or as compassionate as a Jew either.

These writers and Sadducees have no shame and concocted such stories as pleased them to hoodwink the world.

In the first book of Samuel chapter 15 verse 29 it says, 'and the glory of Israel will not lie or repent for he is not a man that he should repent'.

Now we find a reference by the Prophet Samuel stating that God is not a man. How foolish are these compilers of the books of the Bible to fail to remove all the evidence which goes against their contradicting stories?

The First Book of Kings chapter 8 verse 27, King Solomon asks concerning the temple he is building for God, 'But will God indeed dwell on earth. Behold heaven and the highest heaven cannot contain thee, how much less this house which I have built'.

And in Jeremiah chapter 23 verse 23, 'am I a God at hand says the Lord and not a God far off? Can a man hide himself in secret places so that I cannot see him?' says the Lord. Do I not fill heaven and earth?' says the Lord.

Read also Psalm 139 which proclaims God's vastness and omnipresence in the universe.

The word Pagan in the dictionary gives the term also as a Heathen, holding the belief that God exists in natural forces. Nature worshipping, and a Heathen is also someone who does not follow the so called Catholic beliefs, that is their dogmas, creeds and traditions nor do they follow the beliefs of Judaism. The name Pagan and Heathen have been turned into dirty words because they believe God is omnipresent, present everywhere in creation, in nature, in mother earth etc.

Now if God is omnipresent then he must be in all nature. Before Christianity, England was Pagan. It worshipped God in nature and all life. But at the point of a sword we were saved from our ignorance and turned Catholic to worship a man God of the Old Testament and the New Testament, and become saved. Saved from what?

There is a book called 'The World of Jewish Faith' by Myer Dominitz published by Longman in 1980. In this book, Dominitz writes about a Sukkot Festival which is held at the Western Wall, the Wailing Wall of Jerusalem.

On page 35 of Dominitz book he states, 'during the morning synagogue service, people hold myrtle, willow and palm branches in their right hand, and a citrus fruit called Etrog in their left. Etrog is a symbol of the heart, palm of the spinal cord, myrtle of the eye and willow of the lips.

This shows that Jews worshiped God with all their being and plants are waved in all directions to show that God is everywhere.

Did you note the last bit, 'the plants are waved in all directions to show that God is everywhere'? Omnipresent.

Now if God is everywhere, omnipresent and as Samuel states is not a man, doesn't this prove yet again that the Sadducees wrote the books of the Bible with a lying pen in 270 BC, and doesn't it prove they concocted their stories about seeing God face to face, that Moses never saw God face to face, and Abraham never met God and convinced him not to destroy Sodom if fifty righteous men could be found, and whittled the number down to ten?

That Jacob did not wrestle God or even see him?

Adam and Eve never saw God and God did not walk in the garden as he is not a man?

Doesn't it prove he never made Sarah pregnant, nor Rebecca, nor is He the flesh and blood father of the Jewish race?

Doesn't it prove he never had sex with Anna, Mary's mother and doesn't it prove he never had sex with Mary either?

There's more on page 9 of Dominitz book.

In Judaism, no one comes between God and his creatures. Redemption is only possible through God when real repentance is achieved through good deeds.

'No one comes between God and his creatures'.

That means no middle man, no go between, no priest, and man has direct access to God himself as he resides in everyone's heart, and that being so, he won't need to go and see a priest to talk to God, as you have more direct access to God in your own heart than some priest.

Redemption is only possible through God when real repentance is achieved through good deeds.

Isn't my talk on sacrifices all about this? Didn't the Prophets keep telling them that sacrifices were evil and wrong, that all a man had to do was to have a broken contrite heart, be truly sorry for the wrongs he had done, repent and live according to the Ten Commandments which are about loving God with all your being, and your neighbour as yourself and non-violence, then you'll get eternal life?

The Jews love to use sophistries in their talks which comes from the word sophist. A sophist was a member of a Greek philosophy before Plato in 450 to 400 BC. They would teach rhetoric, how to argue a case in a law court, how to make the truth appear to be a lie, and how to make a lie appear to be the truth. To confuse people's minds and make them think they were honest and not deceitful, just like their book of lies.

Isaiah chapter 3 verse 12, 'oh my people your leaders mislead you and confuse the course of your path'. Jeremiah chapter 8 verse 8, 'how can you say we are wise and the law of the Lord is with us? But behold the false pen of the scribes has made it into a lie'.

So why don't the Sadducees and the Catholic Church scrap the book of lies?

Because it is still a powerful weapon to brainwash people with. If they don't use their brains and allow themselves to be conned by the sophistries of the writers of the Old and New Testament. The lies written and portrayed as truths, while the truths were removed and covered up by more lies, but now you have been made aware of their tricks, so you don't have to remain fooled or confused by them anymore.

The book of Leviticus which is all about sacrifices; what to kill, where and how to spring out blood and for what sins, is all a lie, written by the scribes, paid by the rich Sadducees priests who claim that their God gave them to Moses and Moses told the people what God wanted, making Moses the scapegoat for all their lies.

How diabolical is that?

Seeing how the God gave the Ten Commandments for the people to live by, he will not do anything against them as that would make him a hypocrite. God is against killing, 'thou shalt not kill'. He is against lying and cheating, 'thou shalt not lie'. He is against stealing, 'thou shall not steal'.

So why would God sanction the Israelites to go into another country and tell them to go and kill the inhabitants, kill their cattle, the men, women and children and possess the land? Why would he tell them, when he gave the laws thou shalt not kill, steal, or covet your neighbours land, or anything that is your neighbours?

He wouldn't and didn't.

These writings are the sophistries used by the lying priesthood to con the world into thinking and believing that they were God's chosen people and they can get away with murder or anything because they are God's favourite. God has no favourites, otherwise he would be unjust and God is a just God. He did not sanction any breaking of his laws of love. Those who break them will be punished.

It's the law of karma. You reap what you sow, and only what you sow. If you sow turnips, you don't get tomatoes. If you lie and cheat and murder and rob or harm others, you don't go to heaven.

You're not rewarded but suffer for the wrongs you've done. You may think that people get away with murder and can do as they like because they are rich and hide behind the law but the day will come, if not in this incarnation than certainly in a future one or ones, they pay all their debts they owe and not one half penny will be missed.

I strongly believe that the corrupt Sadducees of the Old Testament infiltrated the Christian church and also wrote lies in the New Testament and put them in the mouth of Jesus, just as they did to Moses and also changed the earliest writings of the Gospels, then destroyed the original books so that no trace was left of them and any books or scripts found, even the Dead Sea Scrolls, were corrupted copies left on purpose for future generations to find, just to back up their lying scriptures. They were so cunning and always planned ahead.

In 1956 some clever plan was put in action; the Arab Bible was re-written. The Arabs were supposed to have the same book as the Israelites but the Arab book differs from the 270 BC book.

So, someone re-wrote the Arab book to make it more in line with 270 BC version and flooded the Arab countries with them. This was a big organised job and not the whims of one man. The ruse was discovered, someone spotted the changes in the books and so, all the Arab books around the world were checked and all the new versions were gathered up and burnt.

Why was it done?

Well if the Arab books were all in line with the 270 BC it would give the 270 BC book of lies, more authority and who could then dispute it as they would all be telling the same lying stories.

It states in the Qur'an that the Jews tell lies in their book. It also says the Christians tell lies in their book, not just once but in two or three places it states this.

So, it also backs up what I'm stating, there are lies in the Old and New Testament. There are in fact many lies in both books. They were changed to give the powerful churches more control over the masses and keep themselves in power and luxury while the rest of the world were their slaves, and some today still are. Although many have fallen away from the churches because they were disgusted by them and do realise that there is something wrong with them, their teachings, or just the behaviour of their priests, and instead of suffering punishments like prison sentences, the offenders are just moved to a new parish where they can carry on with their own personal sins and try to brush their past under the carpet and hope the public forgets all about what they've done.

CHAPTER 10

NOAH'S ARK
(The continuation of the transcript of the second CD)

One of the most popular or well-known stories in the Bible is the Noah's Ark story.

In Genesis chapter 6, God is supposed to be angry and repentant of making mankind and is going to kill everyone with a great big flood.

Not a very nice thing for an all loving God to do but the writers don't care that they are telling lies or that it never happened.

We have Noah, his wife, their three sons, and their wives. A total array of people who God is going to save and God is supposed to tell Noah in Genesis chapter 6 verse 14 onwards, 'make yourself on ark of gopher wood, make rooms in the ark and cover inside and out with pitch. This is how you are to make it. The length of the ark, three hundred cubits. Its breadth, fifty cubits and its height, thirty cubits. Make a roof for the ark and finish it to a cubit above, and set the door of the ark in its side. Make it with low, second and third decks'.

Could you make such an ark or ship from that description just being given?

A ship builder probably could but Noah who was probably a shepherd, wouldn't know anything about ship building. It's to be four hundred and fifty feet long by seventy-five feet wide and forty-five feet high.

Can you imagine the number of trees needed to be chopped down made into planks and struts to make the ribcage, and then covered to make the ship, and every joint drilled with wooden pegs knocked into them to keep them secure?

Also, the amount of pitch, how many hundreds or thousands of gallons would be used to make pitch, to use the pitch inside and outside the ark to make it water tight. How many years would it take for such a project?

The wonderful writers of this story do not say but apparently, the animals went into the ark two by two and some animals more than two of their kind.

We re-join the Genesis account in chapter 6 verse 21, 'also take with you every sort of food that is eaten and store it up, and it shall serve as food for you and for them, the animals'.

Noah did this. He did all that God commanded him. God never told Noah to take any drinking water on board, so he never took any, hence they had no water to drink nor did the animals.

How long would they survive without water?

In Genesis Chapter 7 Verse 11, 'in the six hundredth year of Noah's life, in the second month, on the seventeenth day of the month, on that day all the fountains of the great deep burst forth and all the windows of the heavens were opened'.

Verse 16, 'and they that enter, male and female of all flesh, went in as God had commanded him and the Lord shut him in'.

Noah and his family and the animals are shut in the ark by God. Noah is six hundred years old and it's the seventeenth of the second month when this happened. Noah took no water on board for either himself his family or his animal's because God never told him to and he obeyed God right down to the letter.

Now God shuts them in the ark and makes it water tight. It is also air tight. No air can enter it or escape from it. I wonder how long they would survive with no more air than is in the ark. All those animals with big lungs needing oxygen. How long could they possibly survive?

Verse 19, 'and the waters prevailed so mightily upon the earth that all the high mountains under the whole heavens were covered. The waters prevailed about the mountains, covering them fifteen cubits deep, another twenty-two and a half feet.

The story tellers and vendors who concocted the story did not think that sometime, somewhere along the line someone would use their brain and pull this story, as well as other stories in the Bible to pieces. Rain is formed as modern man should know by the sun heating up the ocean, water vaporising, forming the clouds and falling back to earth as rain.

We all know the vast amount of land as above the waters of the world and all the mountain ranges also. You know that Mount Everest is about 1.9 miles above sea level, so how could the rain which comes from the sea, being low lying, ever hope to cover the entire planet over a further height of nearly two miles?

It isn't possible. There is not enough water in the oceans to do that, as rain would wash off the land, form rivers and flow back into the sea. It cannot be done, it is physically impossible, yet people have believed that story in the far past and people even still believe it today.

But people with brains should use their brains and see how absurd and stupid such a story is.

So, this is another flaw in the so-called book called the Holy Bible which claims all scriptures are inspired by God, again calling God or implying that he is stupid or a moron.

Genesis Chapter 7 verse 24, 'and the waters prevailed upon the earth a hundred and fifty days'.

How does the story teller know this when all the people, shut up in the ark with no air no water to drink and no windows in the ark, because God only told him to make a door on the side? They wouldn't even know if it was day or night as they couldn't see the sun, and there being no windows on the ark and they didn't have watches in those days, so how could they tell the passage of time, and how would they know that Mount Everest was covered by twenty-two and a half feet of water?

There is lots of guess work going on here.

Chapter 8 verse 1 to 3, 'and God made a wind blow over the earth and the waters subsided. The fountains of the deep and the windows of the heavens were closed. The rains from the heavens restrained and the waters receded from the earth continually'.

Where would the waters recede to? Where would they go? Was there a bath plug in the earth that someone pulled for the waters to recede into? Wouldn't have all the oceans disappear also, and wouldn't such a large amount of water put out the fires in the inner earth and destroy the electric magnetic field of the earth and cause the earth to become as barren as the moon?

This story gets sillier and sillier.

Chapter 8 verse 4 to 6, 'and in the seventh month of the seventeenth day of the month, the Ark came to rest upon the Mountains of Ararat and the waters continued to abate until the tenth month. In the tenth month on the first day of the month the tops of the mountains were seen'.

How was it possible to know these days and months when they are locked up in the ark without windows to see out of? How was it possible to see how the tops of the mountains were seen?

Seen by who?

Verse 6-7, 'at the end of forty days Noah opened the windows of the ark which he had made and sent a raven forth'.

Now, suddenly, the writers have invented a window!

How convenient.

But that is going against God's commandments. God never told Noah to make a window, he only told him to put a door in one side, and it is written that Noah did all that God commanded him, but now we see he didn't.

Noah's story starts at six hundred years of age, the seventeenth of the second month of that year, now we are at the seventh month and the seventeenth day of the month, when the Ark rests on Ararat and after another forty days Noah opens a window, which magically appeared, making it the twenty-ninth of the eighth month.

Take away seventeen of the second month and we find that Noah and his family and animals have been without water for two hundred and eight days and, before this window appeared, they also had no air for two hundred and eight days.

Do you think they finally realised their mistake and quickly invented a window to keep the story alive and everyone in the ark?

Miracle after miracle, what a time to live in. Where are all the miracles today? Perhaps the scribes have lost their magic pen.

Chapter 8 verse 13 to 14, 'and it came to pass in the six hundredth and first year in the first month, the first day of the month, the waters had dried from the earth and Noah removed the covering of the ark and looked, and behold the face of the ground was dry. In the second month on the twenty seventh day of the month the earth was dry'.

So, the waters dried from the earth. Where did they dry to? Where did they all go?

Maybe back into fantasy land where they came from in the first place.

On the 27th day of the second month in the six hundred and first year the ground was dry. This means Noah and his family and all the animals lived on the ark for 1 year and 10 days without any water to drink.

Another miracle.

But wait, the story isn't over yet. If the whole of the earth was covered with water, wouldn't it all be salted, and wouldn't the soil be covered in salt also? How long will it take for the salt to be gone from the land? Wouldn't all the fresh water also be salted, lakes, ponds, pools, rivers, lochs?

So, after getting off the ark, there is no fresh water to drink, it's all salted. How long would it take for it to rain again and for the rain to wash the salt off the land, off the soil, wash it out of the lakes, ponds, pools and rivers, before you could drink it, and wouldn't all fresh water fish also be dead, killed by the salted water?

So here we have an ark with no water for anyone to drink and after one year and ten days there still isn't any water to drink. So how did any of these people or animals survive?

Another miracle but one written by a false pen as most of the scriptures are.

Back in the days of Noah they did not have any glass. Mirrors were made of polished metal and windows were wooden and solid, you can't see through them, they are just wooden shutters.

So, Noah couldn't have looked out of the window which he never made in the first place. Noah and his wife and their three sons and their wives repopulate the entire worlds from 2400 BC, which was the period of the flood, as some people worked out, from Mount Ararat these eight people made the Japanese, the Polyenes, the Australian Aborigines, the New Zealand Maurois, the black Africans, the yellow Chinese. the American red man, the South American Indian tribes, the Incas, the Aztecs, the white Prussians, the brown Indians of India.

All the tribes of people throughout the world and a vast variety of languages also. All from 2400 BC in such a short period of time. How would Noah get all the animals, which are unique to the Americas both north and south, all the animals which are unique to Australia and New Zealand, and to the British Isles? After all, his ark was stuck on Mount Ararat and he couldn't use that?

So how did he get all these animals there and just as equally important how did he get them on board in the first place?

Another miracle of the lying pen.

The world was flourishing with people and animals all around the world in 2400 BC. It also proved the story wrong. Perhaps you think the story is true but they got their time wrong.

Well, check out the history books and see if you can find it in them.

As I've already stated in 270 BC seventy Jewish emissaries went to the libraries of Alexandria and copied various texts from around the world. They took the story of Atlantis, rewrote it and fashioned Noah's Ark with it.

The sinking of Atlantis took place around 10500 BC. The evidence was later destroyed in the fires of the library which some nice people didn't want certain knowledge, or evidence of the knowledge, to remain intact. There have been many expeditions to Mount Ararat to look for the Ark which never existed in the first place so they are not going to find it.

How can they when the story was fabricated by a lying pen, and billions of people have believed the Noah's Ark story for many years and some people still believe it today. They even believe every word in the Bible and think God was an angry God in the Old Testament and was a man, but eventually he evolved into an all knowing, omnipresent, all loving God and had sex with Mary, and Jesus was his son!

You can lead a horse to water but you can't make it drink.

Likewise, when people hear these recordings and the evidence presented from the Bible, and use common sense to see they'd been lied to.

But unfortunately, a lot of people won't believe their own eyes and ears or use their own brains, and will go on defending the lies of the Bible and the church in case God thinks they're being disloyal to him and send them all to hell, another place which does not exist.

If you think the Bible is true and is the inspired word of God, bring me proof of this. You cannot say your proof is in the Bible because I've shown you proof that it was written with a lying pen, and if that is all the proof that you have, then you are one very sorry excuse for an intelligent human being.

You can fool some of the people all the time, you can fool all the people some of the time but cannot fool all the people all the time. Unless of course you want to go on being fooled and that is your choice. I'm merely showing you the errors of your blind beliefs.

CHAPTER 11

MOSES AND THE TEN PLAGUES OF EGYPT
(The continuation of the transcript of the second CD)

One last story for you to get your teeth into, another one of the most famous stories of the Bible and they've even made a motion picture of it to portray their lying story to further brainwash you with special effects.

I'm talking about Moses and the ten plagues of Egypt which were based upon natural phenomena.

There was a record of these events kept in the libraries of Alexandria concerning a volcanic explosion further up the Nile.

Moses was a psychic that was in touch with the spirit world and people were guiding him. They knew that a volcanic eruption was about to take place because they could see into the future. So, they told Moses to tell Pharaoh to let the Israelites go, otherwise it would rain fire from heaven.

Pharaoh just laughed and refused this request because it was impossible for fire to fall from the sky. But after the explosion which threw rocks for miles, which were on fire, some came down where the Pharaoh lives. Impressed, the Pharaoh told Moses to go, but he changed his mind. The spirit world told Moses to tell Pharaoh that the river was going to turn red, which Moses did. But Pharaoh would not let them go. The river did turn red because of the molten lava and because of the pollution.

Pharaoh was surprised at this scene, also the frogs were leaving the polluted river and the dead fish were floating by, which also brought a plague of flies to eat the dead fish.

Pharaoh relented and told Moses to go. So, Moses and the Israelites left in their thousands.

While Moses and their people were approaching the Sea of Reeds, a smaller part of the Red Sea, Pharaoh received some visitors. The people further up the Nile, who had lived near the volcanic explosion, had lost their houses, farms and crops because of the lava etc. and many were killed in that area.

The survivors went to Pharaoh for help, for food and a place to stay and live. When the people told Pharaoh what had happened and Pharaoh realised the fire from heaven, the Nile turning red, the fish dying and the plague of flies was all natural phenomena and not the God of Moses, or rather Israelites, he was angry. He was absolutely fuming. He realised he'd been tricked by Moses and he wanted his head. He sent his army after Moses and the people, to drag them back. He was going to make a public exhibition of Moses before he killed him.

Back to the Sea of Reeds.

This is run on a tidal system like most rivers connected to the sea.

At high tide the river is up but at low tide the Sea of Reeds is nearly dry and not very deep in parts. Just as luck would have, it Moses and the people crossed the Sea of Reeds at low tide, it being about a foot high, and crossed it easily, but bad luck for the Egyptians who followed Moses, because the tide was changing, and just like the Solway Firth (off the west coast of Scotland) when the tide comes in, it comes in very fast and so the Egyptian army, those who were in the Sea of Reeds got caught up in the rushing, rising tides and drowned. When the libraries of Alexandria were set on fire, the records of the volcanic explosion, which were mentioned earlier, were destroyed and the wonderful story tellers of the Old Testament added a few other plagues just for good measure. So, Moses never parted the Sea of Reeds.

If you were to believe the Bible's account, there was a wall of water upon the right, and a wall of water upon the left. Now if you were to halt the flow of the river, wouldn't the unblocked part just run away to the ocean? Wouldn't there just be one side where the river was blocked?

How many people have allowed themselves to be hoodwinked by this story and still are?

If they use a bit of common sense all these stories would be seen for what they are, political tools to brainwash and control you with, by fear.

If God is the same God as yesterday, today and tomorrow, then it can be plainly seen that he never killed anyone, nor did he have to tell others to kill. God never told the Israelites to go and kill people or steal their land, to give them any promised land in Canaan.

He never told them, to make any animal sacrifices or birds or any other thing to wash away their sins. He never brought the so called ten plagues upon Egypt as I've just explained it. Neither did God send any Angel of Death to the first born male children or cattle. He never told anyone to put blood on door posts so that the Angel of Death would pass them by.

If God is clever why wouldn't he just kill all the Egyptians and give the Israelites Egypt to live in? Wouldn't that have been a better solution?

These fantasy stories were written by a lying pen that proclaim they are God's chosen people and how God did mighty deeds for them and killed their enemies with fire and brimstone in heaven. They frightened others to believe, them and be subservient to them, otherwise they wouldn't go to heaven but burn in hell for all eternity.

As Isaiah said, 'oh my people, your leaders mislead you and confuse the course of your path', and Jeremiah, 'how can you say we are wise and the law of the lord is with us, and behold the false pen of the scribe has made it unto a lie'?

That sums up most of the Old and New Testament, written by lying pens of the priesthood to rule the world and keep you all living in fear and subservient to them, while they live in luxury.

(End of transcript of the second CD)

Of all the systems of religion that ever were invented, there is no more derogatory to the Almighty, more unedifying to man, more repugnant to reason, and more contradictory to itself than this thing called Christianity. Too absurd for belief, too impossible to convince, and too inconsistent for practice, it renders the heart torpid or produces only atheists or fanatics. As an engine of power, it serves the purpose of despotism, and as a means of wealth, the avarice of priests, but so far as respects the good of man in general, it leads to nothing here or hereafter.

Thomas Paine

CHAPTER 12

THE CREATION
(The transcript of the third CD)

In my first two talks I revealed many lies that are in the Old and New Testament and hopefully opened your eyes to see things in a new light. In this one I'm going to reveal God, creation and the meaning of life, and answer the questions which the church never could.

God moulds creation from dark matter. A glove has no life of its own but when you put your hand into it, it comes to life and moves according to your will. When you remove your hand, it ceases to be active. Likewise, with dark matter, it is only activated when God moves into it.

The Bible states in Genesis chapter 1 verse 1 to 2, 'in the beginning God created the heavens and the earth. The earth was without form and void, and darkness was upon the face of the deep. And the spirit of God moved upon the face of the waters'.

The earth was without form and void because it did not exist. It was a part of these waters of the deep. Bhagavad Gita also refers to creation being formed out of water and the Qur'an states that heaven and earth were of one piece. He parted them and made every living thing from water.

It also states He shall roll up the heavens as a scroll. As He began the first creation He shall repeat it. Allah produces creation, then He reproduces it and unto Him you will be returned.

India's books state that God makes creation out of water, sustains it for a while, then dissolves it back into the water and after a while recreates with it again.

Creation is not a one off, but a continuous thing that keeps getting recycled over and over for all of eternity.

Creation is as old as God himself.

This water which the scriptures are talking about is actually the substance called dark matter, it is not water at all. I have seen dark matter. It is made up of minute little black balls.

God shone a light upon this so I could see it. God is pure light, pure consciousness, and is pure energy.

I was in the bodiless state when I was shown this dark matter. This means I was out of my physical body, out of my astral body, and out of my soul body. I was in my natural state of pure consciousness, just like God. Otherwise I would not have been high enough to see these balls of dark matter as they exist above the planes of soul and above the ethers, which the planes of soul are made from.

The ethers are a combination of dark matter and God. God is a vast ball or sphere of pure light and he is pure energy and that energy is neutral. That is, it is both the negative and positive energies of electricity brought together and they are in perfect harmony in the neutral zone.

If you look at a magnet, at one end of the bar there is a positive pole at the other there is a negative pole, but in the middle of the bar it is neither positive nor negative. It is the combination of the two, united in the neutral zone making ether energy, and so is God.

Self-feeding, eternal energy.

God has within him a positive and negative energies, the male and female aspect. It takes both to create with, although they have no sexual organs or bodies, as we have, but they are the father and mother of creation.

Our father and mother God.

When these two come together and unite, the third energy is made and is referred to as the neutral energy, or Christ, the only begotten of the father mother God, the three in one, the one in three.

These references to God were given to mankind a long time ago. Man was very young and could not comprehend a God of pure energy, and so man was told of a God he could relate to and understand, and so a human God was portrayed so that mankind could understand.

Hence, we refer to them as our father and mother God. Years later the mother principal was changed and Mary, Jesus's mother, was portrayed in this role by the Catholic Church, but in ancient days many religions around the world portrayed the Gods as human and they also had Goddesses.

In the Bible, God is portrayed as Father, Son and Holy Ghost. In the Aquarian Gospel by Jesus the Christ by Levi, Jesus told his Disciples that he would send the Comforter to them when he departed the earth, and she would reveal the mysteries of the soul, of life, of death, of immortality, and the oneness of a man with every other man and with God. Then the world would be led to truth, and when she comes, the Comforter, she will reprove the world of sin, and of righteousness, and of judgment and the Prince of carnal life will be cast out. The Comforter, the Holy Breath or Holy Spirit, is divine mother the wisdom aspect of God.

The Catholic Church, and other faiths before it, did not like God being portrayed as a female so they suppressed it and changed this to the Father, Son and Holy Ghost. Just to keep women subjugated and not have any say in religion or politics, as this is a man's world, and Adam was made first and is superior to Eve, as Eve was made from one of Adam's ribs.

Not true of course, another lie in the Bible put there by priests.

So, what happens when God moved in to dark matter?

God is a massive ball of pure, white energy.

But his energy is much higher in vibration than any other planes of soul and higher than ether.

I was shown this from the side of dark matter because, if I was shown it from God's side of pure light, then I would not have seen the change as they would have been hidden by the great light of God.

I saw dark matter start to become lighter in colour, from black and change into grey, then into pure white, which is called ether.

I saw this on the 23rd October 2008 for the first time, and times after this when I was shown the ether in different colours, amethyst being one of them. From the ether, all the elements are made, earth, air, fire and water.

God also showed me the final stages of dissolution of creation when everything is reduced back into the ether and God withdraws from it and it changes from white to grey and back to black and is once again dark matter.

This substance is God's building clay, which he creates the universes from, and all creation.

All the individual spirits, human as well as animals, are alive which has God's spirit in them return to God at the dissolution of the universe as a book from India states as does the Qur'an.

We have two things which are eternal, God and dark matter.

Science recognises the existence of dark matter but maybe not of God. God moves into dark matter, but not all of him. He remains in the neutral zone, self-energising and energises the aspects of himself and dark matter in creation.

That is, he is the positive and negative and the neutral energies in creation.

There are many combinations of these three energies in creation, and the neutral is also used to keep matter and anti-matter separate.

Otherwise you get a big bang.

So, God moves into dark matter, changing these minute black balls into ether and from the white ether comes all the colours of the rainbow. God moves these white balls and makes protons and neutrons and makes atoms. Depending upon how many protons and neutrons are in the atoms will determine what they are going to be. Earth, air, fire and water etc.

He makes the planes of souls, the astral planes and the physical universes. There are many.

God also makes all the forms of life on every plain of life from these elements. In every atom, we see these protons and neutrons flying about and these positive and negative energies which produce electricity and light.

This is the light that lights up every man. The light of the universe etc.

Jesus is said to have said, 'He is the light of the world'. It is this light, this energy, this electricity God, which lights all the atoms of creation. The life-giving energy which is God and is omnipresent in all animate and inanimate things.

In John chapter 1 verse 1 to 5 we read, 'In the beginning was the Word, and the Word was with God, and the Word was God. He was in the beginning with God. All things were made through Him, and without Him nothing was made that was made. In Him was life, and the life was the light of men. And the light shines in the darkness, and the darkness did not comprehend it'.

The Word that was in the beginning is referred to as Om in Indian's holy books. It is the sound of electricity. When you stand near a high-powered electricity cable, especially if it's damp, you can hear the hum of electricity pulsing through the wires. This is the sound, or the word, which creates light, the light in every atom, the light in men also. The light shines in the darkness and the darkness has not overcome it. It cannot, as light dispels darkness.

There is mention in John's gospel, but since people are not fully aware of John's opening remarks, or of dark waters mentioned in Genesis, it passed them by unnoticed and not understood.

God made all creation, the planes of soul, astral planes and physical universes, oceans, rivers, plants, trees etc.

God now scatters seeds of himself onto the planes of soul and man becomes a living soul. This divine seed of God, your true self, is made in God's image, that is, it is positive and negative energy which is united in the neutral. God separates the positive and the negative energies and makes the positive male and the negative female. Now they are two separate consciousness, two aspects of the whole and you can read the symbolic story in Genesis chapter 2 verses 21 to 24.

Mankind is very much as a child on earth and has no understanding, as so far, he has no experiences to fall back upon. They have consciousness, sight, smell etc. but cannot speak as such, because all communication is done by telepathy. As a child on earth, when it starts to crawl and toddle, gets into all kinds of mischief, pulling things out of cupboards, and drawers etc. it's only exploring its environment, not realising that it's causing aggravation and upset to its parents.

Likewise, the young souls are exploring their environment and doing things which, many lifetimes and millions of years later, they will have to put right as ignorance of the law is no excuse. Yet at this stage in life, it is understandable. Later, after many years of living on the planes of soul and exploring, they come to the edge of it where the vibrations are slower and denser.

They step onto the astral plain and become clothed in astral matter, and they see animals having sex, so they thought they'd give it a go, and so with their bodies they took it upon themselves to have sex and the feelings were so intense so beautiful, they were hooked.

They shed the astral body and returned to the planes of soul. But they wanted to experience these feelings again and again. That's when they put on the astral body for a few more times, they could not shed it, and return to the planes of soul. They were stuck in them.

Now this astral body, like the soul body has a mind made up from the ethers of the astral planes and a body of desires, emotions, and this is man's first flesh body, even though it is on a higher vibration than physical matter.

But it is where it began, and you can read the symbolic story of Genesis chapter 3 verse 21, 'and the Lord God made for Adam and for his wife garments of skins and clothed them'.

The garments of skins which clothed them were flesh bodies which covered their soul bodies and now this flesh body with its desires and added carnal nature, becomes man's enemy.

Man is still as a child but is gaining knowledge through mental and emotional experiences. They're starting to learn from the opposites in life of good and bad, positive and negative, happiness and sadness, when its desires are not fulfilled.

Man is a spirit made in God's image, given a soul body, split into two separate beings and now has an astral flesh body. The real man is the consciousness in the heart of the soul body, but man has no real knowledge of himself or his environment. The soul body can think. It has a mind of its own but the spirit mind in the heart can overrule the head, if you listen to it.

Now there is an astral flesh body which can also think and feel and is made up from the elements and puts thoughts into the head of man and manipulates the emotional body to move man into actions of a selfish nature.

A man, being ignorant and who has not yet developed his discriminate faculty, follows the thoughts and emotions as does a blind man being led. Not realising he is doing, and causing, harm to others, because mankind is being selfish, the ethers of the astral planes also slow down and mankind is descending further down the vibrational scale.

Here is a story from the Aquarian gospel of Jesus the Christ by Levi the only true story of the life and teachings of Jesus which has not been corrupted by the lying pen of the priesthood. This extract in the introduction of the book under the heading called Man.

'Time never was when man was not. If life of man at any time began, a time would come when it would end. The thoughts of God cannot be circumscribed. No finite mind can comprehend things infinite. All finite things are subject unto change. All finite things will cease to be because there was a time when they were not. The bodies and the souls of men are finite things and they will change, from the finite point of view the time will come when they will be no more, but man himself is not the body nor the soul. He is a spirit and is a part of God. Creative fate gave to man, to spirit-man, a soul that he might function on the planes of soul, gave him a body of the flesh that he might function on the planes of things that are made manifest'.

Man is a thought of God. All thoughts of God are infinite. They are not measured by time, for things that are concerned with time begin and end. The thoughts of God are from the everlasting of the past until the never-ending days to come and so is man, the spirit man. But man, like every other thought of God was but a seed. A seed that held within itself the potencies of God just as the seed of any plant on earth holds deep within itself the attributes of every part of that special plant.

So, spirit man, a seed of God, held deep within himself the attributes of every part of God.

Now, seeds are perfect, as perfect as the source from which they come. But they are not unfolded into life made manifest. The child in the womb is perfect as the mother is. So man, the seed, must be deep planted in the soil that he may grow and unfold as does the bud unfold to show the flower.

The human seed that came forth from the heart of God was pre-ordained to be the Lord of planes of soul and of the plane of things made manifest.

So, God, the husband man of everything that is, threw forth his human seed into the soil of soul, and growth appeared and man become a living soul, and he became a Lord of all the kingdom of the soul. The plane of soul is but the ether of the spirit plane vibrating not so fast, and in the slower rhythm of this plane the essences of life are manifest.

The perfumes and the odours, the truth sensations and the all of love are manifest, and these soul attributes became a body beautiful. A multitude of lessons man must learn upon the planes of soul and here he tarries many ages until lessons are all learnt.

Upon the boundaries of the plane of soul the ethers began to vibrate slower still and the essences took on a garb. The perfumes and odours and true sensations and the all of love were clothed in flesh and man was clothed in flesh.

Perfected man was passed through all the ways of life and so a carnal nature was full manifest. A nature that sprang forth from fleshy things. Without a fall a soldier never knows his strength and thought must be developed by exercise of strength, and so this carnal nature soon became a fall that man must fight that he might be the strength of God made manifest.

Man is the Lord of all the planes and manifests, of protoplast, of mineral, of plant, of beast. But he has given up his birth right just to gratify his lower self, his carnal self, the flesh. But man will fully regain his lost estate, his heritage, but he must do it in a conflict that cannot be told in words.

He must suffer trials and temptations manifold. But let him know that Cherubim and Seraphim that rule the stations of the sun and spirits of almighty God who rule the solar stars, are his protectors and his guides, and they will lead to a victory.

Man will be fully saved, redeemed, perfected by the things he suffers on the planes of flesh, the astral planes, and on the planes of soul. When man has conquered carnal things, his garbled flesh will then have served its purpose well, and it will fall and be no more. Then he will stand on the planes of soul where he must complete his victories.

Unnumbered souls will stand before the man before the planes of soul. There he must overcome them, every one. Thus, hope will ever be his beacon light, there is no failure for the human soul, for God is leading on and victory is assured.

Man cannot die. The spirit man is one with God, and while God lives man cannot die. When man has conquered every foe upon the planes of soul, the seed will have full opened out, will have unfolded in the holy breath. The garbled soul will then have served its purpose well and man won't need it evermore, and it will pass and be no more, and man will then attain unto the blessedness of perfectness, and be at one with God.

That is the end of that part concerning man on the Aquarian Gospel.

CHAPTER 13

SERAPHIM AND CHERUBIM
(The continuation of the transcript of the third CD)

Here's a little more insight into that part where it states that Seraphim and Cherubim have ruled the stations of the sun, and the spirits will rule the solar stars by his protectors and guides and they will lead to victory.

It is a Cherubim and Seraphim who rule each sign of the zodiac. These are the twenty-four elders who sit around the throne and cast their crowns before God as the Bible states. Each sign of the Zodiac is referred to as an age, and each age lasts about 2160 years. These make sure that the influences of each sign are felt upon earth and that people here learn the lessons they have to teach.

Likewise, the spirits that rule the planets as in your star sign, determine the type of body you have, the diseases you'll be prone to, your character, your likes and dislikes, how you'll feel, the lessons that these star signs teach, who you'll marry etc.

Plus, your own karmatic deaths are all pre-ordained before you come back to earth. Even which star sign you'll be born under to influence you and afford you the best opportunities to learn your lessons under. When the physical body dies you still have an astral body, which is still classed as the flesh body, which it is, it is on a higher vibration but it is still flesh. We have been so conditioned by corrupt religions over many years in our history, who have changed and taken away the ancient wisdom and replaced it with lies and sheer fantasies that mankind, in their ignorance, wonders if they have a soul and a spirit, not realising that they are spirit and eternal and are clothed in a soul body and an astral flesh body, and now believe that they are just a physical body and when it dies that is the end of them.

Back to the Aquarian Gospel of Jesus the Christ by Levi, and see what Jesus says about creation and man.

From God's own record book, we read 'the triune God breathed forth and seven spirits stood before him. The Hebrews called these seven spirits Elohim and these are they who, in their boundless power, created everything that is or was'.

'These spirits of the triune God moved on the face of boundless space and seven ethers were, and every ether had its own form of life. These forms of life were but the thoughts of God clothed in the substance of their ether planes. Men call these planes the planes of protoplast, of earth, of plant, of beast of man, of angel and of cherubim'.

These planes with all their teeming thoughts of God are never seen by eyes of material man in the flesh. They are composed of substance far too fine for human eyes to see, for it is with this substance that the souls of all life on the seven planes are created.

These are the planes of soul and all creatures who learn to see with eyes of soul, may see these ether planes, and, thus, they may learn to see all forms of life.

Because all forms of life on every plain, or thoughts of God, all creatures think, and every creature is possessed of will and in its measure, has the power to choose, and in their native planes all creatures are supplied with nourishment from the ethers of these planes.

And, so it was, with every living thing until the will became a sluggish will and then the ethers of the protoplast, the earth, the plant, the beast, the man began to vibrate very slowly.

The ethers all became denser and all the creatures of these planes were clothed with corset garbs, the garbs of flesh which man can see. And this is course of manifest, which men call physical, appeared. And this is what is called the fall of man. But man fell not alone for protoplast and earth and plant and beast were all included in the fall.

The Angel and the Cherubim fell not. Their wills were ever strong and so they held the ethers of their planes in harmony with God.

Now when the ethers reached the rate of atmosphere and all the creatures of these planes must get their food from atmosphere, the conflict came and that was what finite man has called survival of the fittest, became a law. The stronger ate the bodies of the weaker manifests and here is where the cardinal law of evolution had its rise.

And now man in his utter shamelessness strikes down and eats the beast. The beast consumes the plant, the plant thrives on the earth, the earth absorbs the protoplast. In yonder kingdom of the soul this cardinal evolution is not known and the great work of the masterminds is to restore the heritage of man to bring him back to his estate that he left, when again he will live upon the ethers of his native plane. The thoughts of God change not. The manifest of life on every plain unfold into perfection of their kind and as thoughts of God can never die there is no death to any being of the seven ethers of the seven spirits of the triune God.

Here we have two stories of mankind which really don't go against each other. Man, as seed of God and will grow to perfection and that is why men have the four miracles because it was God or the God part of them which did the miracles from within his own heart.

When mankind reached the planes where atmosphere began and started eating animals, this is the beginning of death of the physical body. Now, which period was it when this began would be hard to pinpoint. Some skeletons of early man maybe as old if not older than three million years ago, but there is a reference in Genesis where mankind is living to an age of nearly one thousand years.

But because of the lowering vibrations, his lifespan has become shorter and shorter. Mankind were telepathic, they used their minds and emotions combined to communicate with each other which is also known as intuition.

We have confirmation of this in the Bible in Genesis chapter 11 verse 1, 'now the whole earth had one language and one speech'.

The people were still telepathic but now they were starting to use words as they were beginning to lose their telepathic abilities, due to the lowering of these vibrations, the slowing down and becoming more materialistic.

After a while maybe many years, perhaps thousands, they eventually lost their telepathic abilities altogether and used words as their means of communication and this, there is a symbolic story in Genesis chapter 11, at a tower of babel where God is supposed to have confused the people on earth and made them speak different languages because they tried to build a tower that would reach up to heaven.

Not a very accurate story, only a symbolic one of how people lost their telepathic ability over a long period of time, and the people spoke different languages depending upon where they lived in different countries around the world. No jealous or angry God at all, just a symbolic story to try and account for the diversity of languages on earth.

You've heard how man was to blame in one story, for the fall of man, here is another by a sage called Ashbina. Taken from the Aquarian Gospel of Jesus the Christ by Levi, chapter 55 and verses 30 to 36, we read, 'seeds do not germinate in light, they do not grow until they find the soil and hide themselves away from light. Man was evolved a seed of everlasting life, but in the ethers of the triune God the light was far too bright for seeds to grow and so man sought the soil of carnal life and in the darkness of earth he found a place where he could germinate and grow.

The seed has taken root and grown full well. The tree of human life is rising from the soil of earthly things and under natural law is reaching up to perfect form. There are no supernatural acts of God to lift a man from carnal life to spirit blessedness. He grows as grows the plant and in due time is perfected. The quality of soul that makes it possible for man to rise to spirit life is purity. There is also a mechanical reason why man descended from the planes of soul down to the astral planes until the earth and all life reached atmosphere and once it reached this lower vibration people started eating meat.

You've heard people refer to the universe as a cosmic clock.

Well clocks have cogs in them. Some cogs move in a clockwise cycle and some in an anti-clockwise cycle, and so do planets.

People speak of vibrational changes and they are expecting the earth to be on a higher vibration in the Aquarian age, yet no one has explained how these vibrational changes happen, until now.

This was given to me by spirit when I read about the Americans during world war two when scientists tried to make a ship undetected by enemy radar. The book is called the 'Philadelphia Experiment' by Charles Burlitz and William Moore, published by Panther Books in 1979.

They had giant generators on board the USS Eldridge and when they switched them on the ship disappeared from physical site. The electromagnetic field had been changed, quickened in vibration and when they switched the generator off it reappeared. This quickening of the vibrations in a short period caused harm to those on board to ship. I won't go into details but you can obtain the book and read it for yourself.

In 'Fingerprints of the Gods' by Graham Hancock, a reference can be found concerning the electro-magnet field of earth on page 484.

Recent advances in the study of Palaeomagnetism have proved that the earth's magnetic polarity has reversed itself more than 170 times during the past 80 million years. This was discovered on the mid Atlantic ridge where the lava has risen and pushes America and Europe further apart causing continental drift.

It is here where some magnetic variations were detected. But what is the cause of these reversals?

While teaching at the University of Cambridge the geologist SK Runcorn published an article in Scientific America which says, 'there is no doubt that the earth's magnetic field is tied up in some way to the rotation of the planet and this leads to a remarkable finding about the earth's rotation itself and the unavoidable conclusion is that the earth's axis of rotation has changed also.

In other words, the planet has rolled about changing the locations of the geographic poles.

Runcorn appears to be envisioning a complete 180-degree flip of the poles.

According to reports published in nature and New Scientist Magazines the last geomagnetic reversal was completed just 12400 years ago, during the eleventh millennium, and scientists expect the next reversal of the earth's magnetic poles to occur around 2030 AD.

The inner core of mother earth's magnetic field is constant and is always pointing magnetic North and South. But the crust of the earth can move out of its normal North and South mode if the weight on the surface of the planet all loses balance.

Let's say through volcanic action. If the crust were to rise in the northern hemisphere, then the weight of the planet's crust would cause it to be top heavy. That being so it would roll over and put the heaviest part at the bottom to regain its balance. That, depending on the speed of its roll, will determine how much damage would be caused to people and animals upon the planet, and such a movement of the crust would cause earthquakes as the tectonic plates will be put under more pressure and the oceans will be upset also, causing tidal waves throughout the planet, killing millions worldwide.

In my earlier talk, I mentioned the sinking of Atlantis and the story being stolen from the libraries of Alexandria and re-written as Noah's flood.

When scientists in Atlantis let the power that they used get out of hand, they could not control it and blew up Atlantis and dematerialised it and it came back down as a deluge of rain and mud, and mostly fell on North Africa as sand, the Sahara Desert and Saudi Arabia also.

It was so violent the earth was moved off its axis and the planet rolled over causing worldwide disasters and the ocean waves killing millions worldwide and this happened about 12400 years ago.

But it was re-written as Noah's flood and they claim it was 2400 BC, ten thousand years after the actual event. There were many crafts used to save people and animals, they even had airships in those days. The technology they had on Atlantis and Lemuria was brought with these people when they landed on earth and civilised mankind and upgraded the human race by genetically altering them to modern day man.

In Genesis chapter 6 verse 4, we have a reference to these men from another planet.

'There were giants in the earth in those days; and after that, when the sons of God came in unto the daughters of men, and they bore them *children*, the same *became* mighty men which *were* of old, men of renown.

These men of old were probably the creators of modern man over 200,000 years ago, but unfortunately the Bible writers claim Adam and Eve were only made some 5000 years ago, which goes against science and common sense.

The ancient Egyptians have, as part of their history, a knowledge which states on page 385 of Hancock's book 'Fingerprints of the Gods', during this time they said there were four occasions when the sun rose out of its wanted place, twice rising where he now sets and twice setting where ne now rises.

It appears that the earth moves its axis roughly every 13000 years, but Runcorn says how it has happened more than 170 times in the past 80 million years, which shows it does not rotate *every* 13000 years and this is due to the weight and balance of the crust.

If the earth is caught up in an ice age, as has happened a few times in earth's history then the planet cannot move around and do 180 degree pull shifts due to the ice holding it in the same electromagnetic vibration for millions of years, and this is shown by the readings from the North Atlantic ridge fault. And as it's just been stated that the Egyptians know of four times the sun rose out of its wanted place, means that because the earth will be the other way up the sun will then appear to rise in the west and set in the east, and also this magnetic reversal upon the earth's crust and all life upon the planet, will take us into a higher vibration into the age of Aquarius and the next time that the earth will do this 180 degree flip will be about 15000 AD and take us into the age of Leo, and once again the sun will appear to rise in the east and set in the west.

The Egyptians had a sphinx by the pyramids to mark the last time the earth rolled over and the sinking of Atlantis.

The sphinx is a lion with a man's head. It stands for the sign of Leo. It also stands for other things but mainly as a marker for the last worldwide disaster and the earth's final descent into solid matter from a higher vibration and where mankind's age also dropped from over 1000 years down to three score years and ten.

Getting back to those beings from another planet who are mentioned in the Bible, are also mentioned in the Vader's, where it is stated that the Gods watched Arjuna and his army with Krishna by his side fighting an opposing army from their metal plates.

If the Indians have saucers as well as plates to eat off, they may well have written that the Gods watched the battles from their metal saucers.

In other words, UFO's.

There are people and tribes throughout the world who have been visited and told by beings who flew down with them. Even the Egyptian Gods, these beings, because of the technology they possessed they were worshipped as Gods and miracle workers. They are being referred to as Angels in the Old Testament when they are in their craft and flying, but when they land and get out they are called men or Lord by the people who see them and talk to them, and it was these whom Abraham met and cooked food for, as did Lot and perhaps used their medical skills and made Sarah pregnant as can happen today where women can still have eggs put into them and have babies even though they are 60 years of age and have stopped having their periods.

Likewise, these are the ones Lot met and it was their technology which destroyed Sodom and Gomorrah. When they taught man about science and men were initiated into their sciences, they were given responsibilities and use of these energies, but as the planet was becoming more materialistic so was mankind and the sect called the 'Sons of Belial' started to take control.

The wise ones saw what was about to happen and so they took the Ark of the Covenant and other instruments of power away from Atlantis. They had many boats around the world and people and animals were put into them and these boats or ships were so designed to stay upright.

After the disasters and the earth's 180-degree axis shift they settled in different parts of the world. Some in Mexico, France and the Pyrenees, some to India, Egypt and other parts of the Middle East.

They built the pyramids, the Sphinx, and opened ministry schools and housed the Ark of the Covenant in the Great Pyramid, where people, after initiation and had passed the tests, were trained to raise the resistance of their nervous system, they were allowed to put their hands upon it and they were not killed. I was such a one.

The physical body was trained to go as high as possible and it was taking these higher energies into the nervous system without killing it. But there is a limit as to what the body can stand. Anyone who had not gone through such spiritual training and touched the Ark of the Covenant would die. They'd be electrocuted, and that was one of the reasons why it was housed in the Great Pyramid, insulated away from the masses.

Later, it was given to Moses when he left Egypt and was carried by two wooden poles made from a tree that did not conduct electricity and it still killed anyone who touched it who was not an initiate and there are a couple of stories in the Bible of people who died when they touched it.

Later, the fabled writers of the Old Testament invented how God told them how to make the Ark of the Covenant and claimed it as their own. They were jealous of the Egyptians and invented the story of God's wrath against them and the ten plagues of Egypt. Yet people believed their story and many still believe it today. The film not long been out called '2012' is said to be based on the Mayan prediction of the end of the world.

It isn't.

It's just about the last days of Pisces and the beginning of the Age of Aquarius. But the planet will go over 180 degrees and the sun will rise in the West and set in the East and the earth will become on a higher vibration.

It won't be a dramatic vibrational change but a gradual one, but quicker than the present one. We are already seeing signs of this quickening as people are now living up to 100 years of age and longer. Some are 115 and it's going to keep on increasing, and it's not all about diet but vibrational changes that are happening on earth.

The earth has been affected by the vibrations of other planets and always has, just like cogs in the cosmic clock, they all turn one way or the other and their radiations affect the earth as well as the other planets in our system.

By the time the earth does another axis shift in about 15000 AD we will be on our way or beyond living to an age of 1000 years of age. To anyone visiting the earth in the future on a lower vibrational wing, all they see will be mountain ranges just as we view Mars and they will think that once upon a time earth probably had life upon it, but if they could raise their vibrations then they'd see that there is still life on earth and that the oceans, rivers, vegetation and people and animals are still here.

It's all a question of vibration. Just as the spirit world is real, where you must leave your body to get there or open your third eye to see it, and that also is very real but on a higher vibration also.

The switching of the earth's electromagnetic field on the earth's crust is responsible for the materialisation of earth from a higher vibration and it will be responsible for the spiritualisation of it also.

In a similar way, the American scientists did this on board the USS Eldridge when they made it disappear and reappear using generators on board to change its electromagnetic structure.

Aliens also use electromagnetism fields on board their craft and by altering the position of the fields they can travel more than 17 times the speed of light as well as they alter their vibrations and appear as solid as we are or disappear as though they were ghosts.

Edgar Cayce made predictions concerning the next earth's axis shift. He was a well-known American seer who has produced a lot of information on Atlantis and did a lot of medical work and healed many people with his knowledge. At the Edgar Cayce Institute in America doctors are still studying his treatments today and they always worked.

He predicted that the top of Europe would change in the blinking of an eye and that most of Japan would go into the sea. California also would go into the sea. The film '2012' mentions and shows California going into the sea and speaks of Japan mostly going into the sea, but does not mention Cayce as their source. Only Runcorn gets a mention.

I've been above the earth in spirit, and seen the bottom part of Italy which looks like a widening boot, I saw where the ankle will be separated from the leg part because of the tectonic plates moving and the ocean coming between them and making it an island of the foot part just above where the ankle would be.

I was warned by spirit in 1980 that there was only 25 years left. I had no idea at the time if this would be the end or the beginning of the end but five days before the 25 years was up a big tsunami struck and many were killed. That was on boxing day 2004.

Since that date there have been many disasters around the world. Tidal waves, hurricanes, earthquakes and the disasters are becoming more frequent.

So, the warning was right about 2005.

It was the beginning of the end of Pisces and the brink of the earth's axis change and many more world disasters will happen and the earth's crusts begins its 180-degree shift. We can expect more earthquakes between the tropics of Capricorn and Cancer. The tectonic plates being disrupted and volcanic eruptions also. Seeing as how the oceans also will be disrupted, drinking water also will get contaminated by salt and become undrinkable.

There are also predications in the book Revelations concerning these times. The mark of the beast 666, if you use numerology the name Fox comes under these numbers. Every American President has been given the nickname of an animal such as Teddy Bear Roosevelt. His nickname was the Bear.

This further future President will be nicknamed Fox maybe because of his is craftiness but now we know his real name or his nickname.

The whore of Babylon mentioned is New York.

In Revelations, chapter 18 verses 2 to 3 and verses 9 to 10 it says, 'she has fallen, Babylon the Great and has become a habitation of demons because all the nations are drunk of the wrath of her immorality and the Kings on earth committed fornication with her and by the power of her wantonness, the merchants of the earth have grown rich and the Kings on earth will mourn and weep for her when they see the smoke of her boiling. Standing far off for fear of her torments saying, 'alas, alas the great city of Babylon, the mighty city. For in one hour has thy judgment come.'

Edgar Cayce made a prediction about America and Russia.

He stated that Russia and America will become friends but later have a fall out and Russia will destroy New York, obviously with a nuclear missile, and afterwards will become friends again.

Cayce says that this is the first major sign to watch for, to know how close the end will be.

A new system will be introduced then as New York is the financial capital of the world, the new system will bring about the mark of the beast. Money being done away with and all wealth will be on a computer, credit cards, ID's etc. by your fingerprints or by scanning your eyes.

This also is in the Book of Revelation.

The Aquarian Gospel of Jesus the Christ by Levi also speaks of these coming days, in chapter 157 verses 20 to 30 we read, 'the conqueror will carry many sons of Abraham away as captive into foreign lands and they who know not Israel's God will tread the highways of Jerusalem until the anti-Jewish times have been fulfilled. But when the people have been punished for their crimes their tribulation days will end'.

These times are being fulfilled.

The sacking of Jerusalem in 70 AD, the scattering of the Jews to many lands, the Second World War and the Germans punished for their crimes.

'But lo, a time will come when all the world will rise like gladiators in a ring and fight just for the sake of shedding blood and men will reason not, they will not see, nor care to see a cause for carnage, desolation, thefts, and they will war with friend or foe'.

'The very air will seem to charge with smells of death, and pestilence will follow close upon the sword, and signs that men have never seen will then appear in heaven and earth, and sun and moon and stars. The seas will roar and sounds will come from heaven that men can never comprehend, and these will bring distress of nation with perplexity. Hearts of the strongest men will faint in fear and expectation of the coming of more frightful things upon the earth.

But while the conflicts rage on land and sea the prince of Peace will stand upon the clouds of heaven and say again, 'peace, peace on earth, good will to men', and every man will throw away his sword and nations will learn war no more'.

'And then the man who bears the pitcher, the sign of Aquarius, will walk forth across an Ark of heaven, a sign and cygnet of the Son of Man will stand forth in the eastern sky. The wise will then lift up their heads and know that redemption of the earth is near'.

In the book of Revelations chapter 6 verse 12 to 14 we read, 'and I saw when he had opened the sixth seal, there was a great earthquake and the sun became black as sackcloth of hair and the whole moon became as blood, and the stars of heaven fell upon the earth as a fig tree sheds its unripe figs when they're shaken by a great wind, and heaven departed as a scroll that was rolled up and every mountain and islands were moved out of their places'.

These verses from Revelations are about the earth's crusts 180-degree movement and has been upside down. The heavens which are the stars cannot be rolled up as a scroll but when the earth is on its 180-degree axis shift it will appear as though the stars are moving but it is actually the earth's crust that's moving and not the stars or heavens, and all of them, mountains and islands are moved out of their place and are facing in a new direction and upside down. What is the cause of the earth's 180-degree flip over?

In Revelation chapter 8 verse 8 will read, 'and the second angels sounded and, as it were a great mountain burning with fire was cast into the sea, and the third part of the sea became blood.'

It was on the national news BBC 1 at 9 o clock on Wednesday 11th March 1998 that astrologers had been monitoring the path of asteroids which are between Mars and Jupiter.

It was stated that the earth was struck by three comets or asteroids 214 million years ago. One hit France, one hit Western Canada and one hit Quebec which obviously wiped out practically all life on earth. And 65 million years ago, another one struck the earth and wiped out the dinosaurs.

The news gave the findings of these astronomers who are monitoring the paths of asteroids and the earth's orbit using a computer. They have discovered that one would pass close to the earth in 2004 and that the earth would be hit by one in 2028.

After that startling news the phone lines were jammed by the panicking public and so the government allayed their fears by telling them that it would not hit the earth at all but pass close by it.

This was accepted by the public but was it the truth?

Are the governments around the world preparing for such a hit just like the film '2012' and building gigantic ships to save some of the mankind and animals also and building safer bunkers underground just for the chosen few? We'll have to wait and see.

The mountain of fire from Revelations can only be a meteorite which strikes in the Atlantic Ocean just above the Gulf of Mexico. I worked this out, as my brother when he was younger, had recurring nightmares. He kept seeing the ocean coming over the opposite hill towards our house and this is over 500 feet above sea level. I drew a line from our place to where the ocean was coming from and took it to the mid-Atlantic just above the Gulf of Mexico, and such a strike would cause the earth to topple over, cause tidal waves, pollute drinking water, and will it be in 2028 as the astronomers say?

And, Runcorn predicts a complete reversal of the axis in 2030.

Are we on the brink and don't have much time left?

Revelation chapter 21 verse 1 to 4, 'and I saw a new heaven and a new earth; for the first heaven and the first earth passed away and there was no more sea, and I, John saw the holy city, new Jerusalem coming down out of heaven from God, made ready as a bride adorned for her husband. I heard a great voice from heaven saying, behold the dwelling of God is with men and He will dwell with them and they will be His people and God himself will be with them and be their God, and God will wipe away every tear from their eyes and death shall be no more. Neither shall there be mourning, nor crying, nor pain anymore. For the former things, have passed away.'

A new heaven and earth.

The earth is upside down and is different, it's new, and your view of the heavens the stars is also different, it's new also. Hence a new heaven and earth. This is also a new Jerusalem but it's not descending from heaven it is ascending, going up in vibration being spiritualised.

The dwelling of God with Man is not a physical flesh and blood God, for such a God does not exist. It means men will become conscious of God dwelling in their hearts and everybody will become more loving and live for each other rather for just themselves. For it is God within them who will make them happy and more loving towards all life. When it says the sea is no more, it is not speaking about the ocean but the sea of human life, as humanity is no longer as vast, as many around the world have died owing to such worldwide disasters and the fourth verse about God wiping away tears and death being no more and neither shall there be mourning, means that people will understand that death of the physical body is not the end of life, that your loved ones live on in a higher vibration in the spirit realms and that you can see and communicate with them, so mourning will be no more.

(*The Seventh Principle of Spiritualism 'Eternal Progress open to every Human Soul'*).

In the Aquarian Gospel by Jesus the Christ by Levi chapter 162 verse 6 to 10, Jesus is speaking to his disciples.

'There are a multitude of things yet to be said, things that this age cannot receive because it cannot comprehend but, lo, I say, before the great day of the Lord shall come the Holy breath will make all mysteries known. The mysteries of the soul, of life, of death, of immortality, the oneness of a man with every other man and with his God, and then the world will be led to truth'.

When she has come, the Comforter, she will convince the world of sin and of the truth of what I speak and of the rightness of the judgment of the just and then the prince of carnal life will be cast out'.

And hasn't my talk been about revealing these mysteries to you?

(End of the transcript of the third CD)

Do you think all of God can be put into a few pages in one book? Do you think that when that book was finished, He had no more inspiration for His children? Do you think you have come to the end of His power when you have turned the last page of your Bible?

Silver Birch

CHAPTER 14

THE SEVEN PRINCIPLES OF SPIRITUALISM

The Fatherhood of God.

The core belief of the religious philosophy of Spiritualism is the acceptance of a Divine Energy. This force, whatever name given to it, has created all there is and sustains all its creation. The 'Spirit of God' exists within and around everything. It is within all of us: we are all children of God so are part of one family. We acknowledge God as our Father.

Andrew Jackson Davis perceived God as an Eternal Spirit which is omnipresent in the entire universe. Man, himself is an individualisation of this Spirit which expresses itself in unchangeable laws. Harmonious co-operation with these laws leads man towards a conscious unity with God.

God is the Father Spirit of the great universal Brotherhood of Man.

In "More Spirit Teaching", transmitted through the mediumship of William Stainton Moses, the spirit communicators described God as the informing, energising Spirit, permeating all. The word Father is the true concept of a God of love, perfect and perpetual, who knows no distinction of race or creed.

The guide Silver Birch declared; 'The Great Spirit is infinite and you are parts of the Great Spirit. We preach the gospel of the Spiritual brotherhood of all peoples, with the Great White Spirit as the common Father'.

The Brotherhood of Man.

We are all part of the universal creative force and therefore one family in God. The operation of true Brotherhood throughout the world would create betterment to the lives of many, bringing equality, security and peace. Spiritualists try to understand the needs of others and help all people regardless of race, colour or creed.

This principle constitutes the essence of religion in practice. Without this principle, religion would be mere phrase mongering. He that serves his neighbour serves God. There is no material advantage in serving your neighbour, but there is the blessing of the spirit. The greatest incentive to love and service is the inequality of life.

Spiritualism proves that service is not unrewarded, and establishes beyond doubt that only by service can spiritual progress be made. This does not follow that service should be undertaken for the sake of personal spiritual advancement. On the contrary, it is essentially the spirit in which the service is given, that spirit of pure unselfishness which enhances the soul. Spiritualism also proves that spiritual qualities are the only permanent treasures of life.

The Communion of Spirits & the Ministry of Angels.

Communion with divine energy is a natural and essential part of existence. Communication between Spirit itself and its creations is an inbuilt ability. Spiritualists use this ability for communication directly, or via a medium, between those in the spirit world and ourselves. This is not supernatural; it is a normal activity. The main purpose of communication with the spirit world is to provide the evidence which supports our philosophy.

The Communion of Spirits, is often considered to be the key principle of Spiritualism. It brings out, in sharp contrast, the basic difference between materialism and spiritualism as a philosophy and between Christianity and Spiritualism as a religion, because of our claim to hold communion with departed spirits. Our demonstrations of proved survival have transformed philosophy from a theory into a reality and religion from a creed into a living experience.

We have now proved, consistently and continuously, for a period of well over one hundred years, that those who die in this material world continue their life without break or interruption in another world, another dimension, which intermingles with our own. Not only do they return to communicate with us, and so prove their survival, but they also, for a period, spend a considerable part of their time helping and guiding us in our earthly problems. We too are essentially spirit, and that vital part of us, which we call the subconscious, is sensitive to spirit influence. Many of us, therefore, although not conscious of the influence of spirit, are nevertheless spirit guided. The spirit inspired mental impressions received by the subconscious will filter through to the conscious level and influence, in varying degrees, the thoughts and actions of the recipients.

In certain individuals, called sensitives, there is a close relationship between the conscious and subconscious levels to such an extent that they are more directly aware, through the extra-sensory perceptive faculties of their spirit body, of the 'finer vibrations' - the different frequency of spirit thought and form, thus making it possible for them to communicate with the spirit people.

Our communication brings us precious and vital knowledge of our immortal natures and eternal destiny. In our communications, we learn that those who have passed on have not changed, except in the physical vehicle through which they express themselves. Their interests and desires, loves and hates, wisdom and stupidity remain identical the moment after final separation from the body has been effected. New laws of a new world however must be learned. New problems, trials and joys await the unfoldment of their spirits.

This realisation helps us to understand the continuity and evolutionary aspects of all life and which practical expression leads us to draw ever nearer towards complete unity. It teaches us to serve in harmony with the Supreme Spirit which expresses itself in us and gives us life. No religion has ever revealed such a clear relationship between our individual lives and their divine source. The Ministry of Angels brings enhanced wisdom to enlighten the individual, society and the world in which we live. This includes those who are dedicated to the welfare and service of mankind bringing inspiration guidance and healing.

The Continuous Existence of the Human Soul.

Spirit is part of the 'Creative Force' and thus indestructible. Energy cannot be destroyed; it can only change its form. After death, the physical body is left behind whilst the soul continues to exist in a different dimension that we call the spirit world. The individual personality continues unchanged by the event we call 'death'.

The philosophy of Spiritualism asserts that man has a continuous spiritual existence which extends beyond his physical life into eternity. Our special mission, as a progressive movement, is to propagate this conception to a world which has been bereft of a responsible spiritual leadership, and is overshadowed by the narrowness and selfishness of a materialist outlook.

All great modern religions teach the idea of some future spiritual state in heaven or hell but their teachings have failed to produce any fundamental or lasting influence in the lives of the majority of the people. This is largely because they have failed to satisfy the demands of the present-day realists who require facts to support theories.

Spiritualism can prove to the individual the fact that life is continuous by demonstrating the return of those who have passed to the Spirit World. This great truth is of the greatest spiritual value, because it profoundly revolutionises our outlook on life and consequently our behaviour.

We realise that our strategy of life must be determined by the broader conception of an eternal destiny, and not by the narrow limits of material life. Spiritualism reveals that we are all part of the Supreme Cosmic Spirit, which is the life principle of the Universe and that we are indestructible parts of the eternal whole.

As spirits, we incarnate into this material world, utilising a suitable vehicle - a physical body - which makes us aware of our physical environment and gives us expression. We incarnate to be of service to God and to gain self-experience. We give in service and receive in spiritual progress and by so doing bring ever greater powers and virtues within the orbit of our expanding influence. At physical death when the material vehicle which houses the soul decays and dies our dynamic spirit, an infinitesimal part of the Supreme Spirit, will automatically utilise another vehicle more suitable for its expression in the next level of existence.

As the spirit evolves, its vibrations become finer and it automatically 'dies' to live again on yet another level, another dimension. In each succeeding level of its existence it will be housed in a vehicle which is suitable for its needs at that level. The indwelling spirit becomes aware of its environment and can express itself only through the body which houses it. We progress then from one level to another in eternal duration, assuming ever-greater responsibilities in the supreme plan of evolution and progress.

Personal Responsibility.

In His wisdom, God has given us enormous potential; we can use that potential to improve our own lives and the lives of others. We have the ability to make decisions throughout our lives as we see fit. What each of us makes of our life is our Personal Responsibility no one can replace or override that right. No other person or influence can put right our wrong doings.

In sharp contradiction to the Christian principle of the 'vicarious atonement', we assert that everyone is personally responsible for his or her own thoughts and actions. 'Whatsoever a man soweth, that also shall he reap'.

Spiritualism asserts that if you transgress the Laws of Nature you will suffer in proportion to your transgression.

Unless a man can conquer his own evil tendencies, banish evil from his life, and make personal atonement for his own sins, by his thoughts and actions, he cannot achieve spiritual progress.

Unless we face up to the reality that all the evil or negative effects of our actions and thoughts remain with us and indeed affect those with whom we come in contact; until by our efforts we change them, we shall never make real spiritual progress. We shall merely live a life of spiritual self-deception, only to come to a grim realisation of our mistakes when ultimately, we arrive in the Spirit World. This is no theological postulate but is based on evidence and experiences of the spirit people themselves.

In our principle of Personal Responsibility, we have a moral stimulus for men to lead a better life, to desire brotherhood in their mutual relationships, to do good for the sake of good and to live in harmony with God.

Compensation and retribution hereafter for all the good and evil deeds done on earth.

The sixth Principle expresses the natural law of cause and effect. This law operates now, on earth, as well as in the spirit world. As we move through life making choices, the outcome of those choices affects our soul growth. When we leave this earthly life, there will be no divine judgement. We will have the opportunity to reassess, take stock and decide what might have been done differently.

This principle merely gives man an opportunity to right any wrongs he has done to others during his lifetime on earth and in his life in the world of Spirit. When we say that there will be compensation and retribution hereafter for all the good and evil done here, we mean that as we live this life, we are determining the course of our future life in the Spirit World. If we do evil, or neglect our cultural development, we are merely developing our souls in such a way as will demand a period of painful struggles to undo and amend what we have neglected to do according to the opportunities accorded to us whilst on earth.

On the other hand, if we have lived good lives, loved our neighbours, and used our opportunities for intellectual progress we will enjoy the advantages which are accrued from our earthly efforts in the form of spiritual advancement and happiness in the hereafter. In other words, we set in motion causes which are carried forward from this life and have their effects in the next.

Life is the unbroken eternal struggle towards greater love and wisdom. The extent to which we can make the effort here relative to our inherited endowments, environment, destiny and opportunities, determined the degree of harmony and happiness which we will obtain in our future spiritual life. This is a natural law of life and operates in proportion to what is potential in our nature.

Our souls are forged in the fire of experience, but none of us is called upon to accomplish the impossible. Each has his appropriate part to play in the Universal Plan. Some have mighty tasks, others humble assignments but all is in accordance with the nature of universal justice which in its perfect operation ensures that spiritual progress and happiness is the equal opportunity of all spirits. Spiritual progress which we are told is not in some inconceivable heaven, but is simply a state of consciousness within, where our judge is our conscience.

Life is one continuous unfoldment of spirit in which there is action and reaction, compensation and retribution, both here and hereafter.

From this, a philosophy emerges which reveals a purpose in life, and gives a satisfactory explanation of our existence.

Eternal Progress open to every human soul.

Eternity does not begin at death; Progress is open to all now! Any action, or intent to change, to promote soul growth and progression, creates a positive reaction. There will always be the opportunity to develop and move forward, no one is ever deprived of the all-embracing love of God.

To progress is to constantly aim for higher spiritual achievements, and as we do so we realise that the accomplishments of yesterday are soon outmoded, and new victories must be won. The old, however, invariably resists the birth of the new, and what was once progressive, now tends to become contradictory and retrogressive, setting in motion forces of disharmony which we recognise as negative influences. Within each one of us there is a constant struggle between what we are and what we should be.

Our primitive animal instincts hold us down to the material sensuous plane. Our Spiritualist philosophy urges us to higher spheres of consciousness. These opposing forces struggle within us, and often it is with difficulty and pain that we prevail against the temptation of the flesh; but those pains are the birth pangs of progress.

Progress is never easy, and great progress demands sacrifice, but our spiritual blessings are in proportion to the efforts we make, stimulating finer vibrations within our souls which raise us ever higher in the great divine spiral of spiritual progress, from sphere to sphere in eternal duration.

Our vast Spiritualist literature contains overwhelming evidence and teachings regarding our eternal future, based upon the personal experiences and knowledge of those now living in the higher spheres of spirit life. God is eternal and therefore the Universe. As we are indivisible parts of God, we are also eternal. This does not necessarily mean that we existed prior to birth as we now find ourselves or that we shall continue eternally in our present form of spiritual existence. One thing is certain; a path of eternal progress lies before us.

CHAPTER 15

MY INTRODUCTION TO SPIRITUALISM

It was 1986 when I first began attending Croydon Spiritualist church on Sunday mornings, listening to the philosophy and the messages being given from the church platform, mainly to other people in the congregation. I did receive the occasional message but could never really relate to them, but this did not deter me from attending because I'd heard other people's messages and realised that the evidence of life after death was quite apparent.

I had hesitantly entered the church but was soon made to feel at ease with the warm welcome I received from the stewards at the door. Any thoughts I might have had that there was something odd about Spiritualists were unfounded and I soon realised that those I encountered over the following weeks and months were friendly, helpful, caring and above all open minded. There was no dogma attached to their religion and freedom of interpretation was encouraged. I certainly felt 'at home' in this church.

During the summer of 1987 I attended a series of six lectures on the various aspects of Spiritualism. These were about the Seven Principles of Spiritualism, the philosophy of Spiritualism, different types of mediumship, the different organisations representing Spiritualism, Spiritual healing, and the running of the church.

I attended each one and due to my interest I was invited to join the church development circle run by the then Vice President, Pat Robertson.

The circle included a good mix of people having various degrees of experience of Spiritual development, from novice to experienced and this enabled everyone to learn from others in the group and be inspired by their progress.

During my time in the circle I made many friends, many of whom have remained friends to this day. Indeed, some of them became committee members and still work with great commitment to ensure the smooth running of the church.

During the regular circle meetings, which were held on Monday evenings, I was taught how to meditate and consequently, how to become less aware of 'self'. This enabled me to gradually become aware of 'outside influences' which initially I found difficult to accept.

At first I became aware of images appearing in my mind that appeared to have no relevance to anything, but under the guidance of the circle leader and others, I was soon made to believe that what I was being shown were images put into my mind by people living in the Spirit world who wished to make their presence known and who wished to communicate through me to others in the circle.

The hardest thing for me to accept was that this was genuine Spirit communication and that my lack of trust was preventing me from accepting this truth. The result was that I failed to pass on what I was undoubtedly seeing, to those in the circle for whom the message may have been appropriate.

It took me a very long time to understand that the purpose of the circle was to practice mediumship without any fear of being wrong and it was only by saying aloud what I was being shown, that I would allow other circle members to accept that the communication may make sense to them and they would respond accordingly.

Once that acceptance became second nature the messages tended to flow more easily and information was communicated to the recipient from their loved ones in the Spirit world.

Another purpose of the development circle was to practice Spiritual healing. This is the act of laying on of hands while requesting that the healing energy may flow from Spirit, through me, to the patient.

Again, this took me a while to understand, but it was explained to us that we are Spirits with a temporary body, and it is when the body dies the Spirit lives on. It was therefore explained that the healing energy was passed from Spirit, through Spirit, to Spirit, the 'healer' being a passive channel through which the energy would flow.

I received many compliments from other circle members, saying that when I gave them healing, the energy felt quite powerful and that my hands became very warm and felt as though they were vibrating or pulsating while they were placed on the patient's shoulders.

One day a request came from the church healing leader for any help that could be given at the healing services because there were often far more patients attending than the healers could cope with. So, I put myself forward to help since I appeared to be a very open channel for the healing energies to flow.

I then began attending the healing service on Thursday evenings, but only within the constraints of my personal life which obviously included my family commitments as well as my work commitments.

Healing must always be considered as a complimentary therapy and a cure can never be suggested, but over the many years of my experience I know of many positive outcomes for patients who had previously been told by the medical profession that no more could be done for them. Often as a last resort patients would attend the church for Spiritual healing and find the symptoms of their illness gradually improving after several weeks of attendance.

It is often the case that if Spiritual healing does not bring about a 'cure', the patient will find peace, with a greater acceptance of their fate and therefore, their passing will be much more peaceful than might otherwise have been the case.

To that end, healing can never be termed as having failed because the patient will certainly have become more relaxed through receiving healing. In addition, there are no harmful side effects.

Returning to the subject of mediumship, I have been asked how mediums receive information from the Spirit world. There are three forms of communication and mediums use one or more of these while receiving communication. These are often termed as the 'three 'C's, clairvoyance, clairsentience and clairaudience. I have heard it said that there is a fourth, 'clairvaguence' which is a term used to describe 'messages' that give no specific information about the communicator and therefore fail to prove life after death, which is the sole purpose of mediumship.

Clairvoyance is described as 'clear seeing' and is probably the most common method of receiving communication. I describe it as seeing images in my mind which were not visible to me before I began my mediumship at a service, and therefore I accept that these images were put into my subconscious by somebody wishing to communicate to somebody in the congregation. It is only by saying out loud what is being shown that the next 'image' will unfold allowing a steady flow of information to continue and for the communicator to describe aspects of his life before he passed to the Spirit world.

Obviously, it is the responsibility for the medium to interpret these images correctly and to realise that if the recipient of the message is unable to understand what the medium is describing, it could be because of the medium misinterpreting what he is being shown.

A simple example of this would perhaps be the medium being shown a rose and suggesting that the communicator liked roses or that a single rose has some relevance, but it could also suggest that the name of the communicator is Rose or that the name Rose has some significance to the recipient of the message. It is only through experience that the medium will learn to understand the significance of the message, while at the same time understanding that it is not for the medium to understand what the message is about, only the recipient.

Clairsentience is a form of communication where the medium senses things about the communicator in the form of pain in a part of the body, or perhaps sensing various types of emotion, sadness or joy, which will have some significance to the recipient of the message. If the communicator was known to have a happy go lucky personality, or was known to be depressed, the medium should be able to pick that up using clairsentience and pass on that aspect of the communicators personality. This would be considered very good proof of who the communicator is.

Clairaudience is a term used to describe a medium's ability to hear subjectively what the communicator saying. This enables the medium to not only describe the tone of voice the communicator had, but also to hear the spoken word, music (suggesting the communicator liked music) as well as sounds that might suggest something relevant to the recipient.

It must be stressed at this point that mediumship does not include making predictions, giving lifestyle advice or any similar information. That is the work of a Psychic, who tends to read the body language and mannerisms of an individual to give a reasonably accurate description of their personality and suggest certain things that may be relevant to that individual's life but does not give any proof of life after death.

CHAPTER 16

SPIRITUAL HEALING

As long as man ignores natural methods of healing and persists in using animals, who were not placed on earth for that purpose, he will fail to promote health and well-being.

Silver Birch

No doubt you will have seen, heard or read something which refers to this subject, for it has certainly received a great deal of publicity in recent years.

In this chapter, it is intended to clear up some of the confusion you might have, and present the rational Spiritualist standpoint.

We refer to "Spiritual" Healing, not "Faith" Healing. Sympathy with and understanding of the ideas of healing can be a great help, but many of the cases dealt with by healers involve those who do not have faith; babies, those too weak or too ill to be concerned with faith, those who seek help as a last resort, and animals.

Our contention is that this healing is a natural activity. You do not need faith for the X-ray to work on you, or the drug to ease your pain, or for the dentist to be able to fill the cavity in your tooth or for the doctor to be able to remove your appendix.

Of course, we do not understand the workings of Spiritual Healing as well as we understand the workings of the nervous system, or the blood circulatory system or similar bodily functions. Because of this, no healer can or should guarantee a cure. The healer will try to bring about a cure; if this cannot be achieved he may well be able to ease the discomfort produced by the problem. Where he feels that medical help is required he should say so.

Sometimes he may realise that there is virtually nothing to be done other than ease the passing of the patient, this itself being of great help to both the patient and his family.

Having said all that, it must be pointed out that Spiritual Healing has achieved remarkable results.

It is achieved by co-operation between the healers and those from the 'Spirit World' who work together to use natural, spiritual force. Using this force, countless individuals have been helped; often it is a gradual reduction and eventual removal of the cause of the problem. What must be stated emphatically is that however spectacular the result, **it is not a miracle**.

The Spiritualist understands that miracles would transgress natural law; healing, or any other aspect of mediumship, never does this.

Disease and illness always have a cause; they are never punishment for 'wrong doing'.

There are two main areas of healing: 'contact' and 'absent'.

Contact healing (often referred to as the 'laying on of hands') requires the healer to be with the patient, administering healing in a simple, dignified manner.

Absent healing allows those unable to attend to be assisted, as well as those unaware that the healing is taking place.

Most Spiritualist centres hold healing sessions, often on several occasions each week. There are also many sanctuaries dedicated to healing. It should be stressed at these sessions that the mental attitude of the person can have a great effect - relaxation and positive thought can go a long way to remove or prevent many of the illnesses to which we are prone.

Healing can be work which gives satisfaction; but even if you never become an active healer you can still, in your own quiet moments add the strength of your thoughts, goodwill and love to the healing forces around all of us, that all those in need might reap the benefit.

CHAPTER 17

NATURAL LAW

The scientists' religious feeling takes the form of a rapturous amazement at the harmony of natural law, which reveals an intelligence of such superiority that, compared with it, all the systematic thinking and acting of human beings is an utterly insignificant reflection.

Albert Einstein

As well as the Seven Principles of Spiritualism there have been many examples of trance mediumship involving individuals in the spirit world communicating through a medium who is sufficiently developed to enable him his mind and body to be taken over enabling them to speak about life in the spirit world, to which we will all one day go, and to speak about the problems of the physical world, such as warfare, poverty, hunger, homelessness to mention just a few.

One such communicator was Silver Birch who spoke through the mediumship of Maurice Barbenell, a young newspaper reporter who accepted an invitation to attend a séance at the home of Hannen Swaffer, a prominent English journalist in the twentieth century.

Barbenell's intention was to write a report in his local newspaper ridiculing Spiritualism but he apparently fell asleep. On awakening he was told that he had not been sleeping but had been in a state of trance and an individual named Silver Birch had spoken through him and had given some wonderful philosophy of religion.

Barbenell continued to attend the circle and, over time produced several volumes of Spirit teachings given by Silver Birch which were published by the Spiritual Truth Press.

I am indebted to The Spiritual Truth Foundation for permission to reproduce some of these teachings which are specifically about 'natural law' which in the opinion of many Spiritualists represent a more logical explanation of the creator we call God, or the Great Spirit.

I also include quotations from my own guides who have spoken through me at trance demonstrations.

THE INESCAPABLE NATURAL LAW

The law which you call Spiritualism is part of the natural law. The Great Spirit has ordered the universe to be ruled and to be expressed through unchanging laws. These laws control every facet of universal activity. Nowhere in the whole universe, whether in those regions known to you or in that much larger portion which is beyond human reach, is there absence of natural law.

You are responsible for everything you think, say and do. As your body is the means by which you express yourself on earth, you must give it the attention that is essential for it to perform its labours. It is a wondrous, most complex, remarkable organism, far more intricate than anyone can construct on earth. It is a marvel of apparatus, but must have attention.

If you live in harmony with the natural laws you do not have illness, disease, or ailments. These are due to disharmony. Break the law and pay the price. Live within the law and reap the benefit.

'Nothing is outside the orbit of natural law. The seasons follow one another, the earth rotates on its axis, the tide ebbs and flows. Whatever seeds you plant, what will grow is contained within it; it will be true to its nature. Law reigns supreme. Every new discovery, whatever it may be, wherever it may be, is controlled by the same natural law. Nothing is forgotten, nothing is overlooked, nothing is neglected. What is this power responsible for it? It is infinite. It is not magnified man, the Jehovah of the Old Testament. It is not a deity who is full of vengeance and sends plagues because of displeasure. It is not a capricious, wrathful deity. History and evolution show that the world slowly moves forward, upward, revealing that the power behind it is beneficent. So gradually you get this picture of infinite love and wisdom that rule all, that governs all, that direct all. And that I call the Great Spirit'.

THE LAW
If you are faced with war, there will be many who say: 'why doesn't the Great Spirit stop it? 'Why doesn't the Great Spirit prevent it?'

Yet all the time, the people of your world are to blame if they choose to ignore His laws. Do not think that your world can escape the consequences of its actions. We cannot alter the law. What has been sown must be reaped. You have sown selfishness; you must reap the results. Pride, jealousy, envy, greed, malice, distrust, suspicion – all these things, when they fructify, produce war, distress and discord.

CAUSE AND EFFECT
The law is perfect in its operation. Effect always follows cause with mathematical precision. No individual has the power to alter by one hair's breadth the sequence of cause and effect. That which is reaped must be that which is sown, and the soul of every individual registers indelibly all the results of earthly life. He who has sinned against the law bears on his own soul the results of his earthly action, and there will be no progress until reparation has been made for the sinful deed.

If effect did not follow cause, your world, the universe and the vast cosmos would be chaotic. Th Great Spirit, God, the Deity, the Supreme Power, would not be the summit of love, wisdom and the perfection of all that exists.

94

The universe is ruled by divine justice. If at a stroke, by reciting some words said to have some religious and spiritual significance, you could obliterate the results of some wrong you have done, then that would be a criticism that the natural law was not perfect in its operation, but unjust because you could change its pattern.

NATURAL LAW

All law is part of one vast law. All works in harmony because all is part of the divine plan. The lesson of it is that men and women throughout the whole world of matter must seek their salvation by working it out in their daily lives, and abandon all the false theology which teaches that it is possible to cast on to others the results and responsibilities of your own actions.

Man is the gardener of his own soul. The Great Spirit has provided him with all that is necessary for it to grow in wisdom, grace and beauty. The implements are there, he has but to use them wisely and well.

Silver Birch

I can know of no other greater use of our spiritual energies than to help other people. In so doing you help yourselves, as you know, the more you give the more you shall receive.

God the father, the father of all creation the father of all you perceive, of all you touch, all you feel, and all that you see.

God is your father and you are his children. You have no label, no attachment to any other. You are guided by your thoughts. Your thoughts are energy; your energy is at one with God, for God is energy.

Some say God is love, love is energy. You give out energy when you speak of love, when you care for your friends, your loved ones. When you hug, when you touch, you feel, you listen, you speak with love. You are using God's energy.

Fine Feather

Peace is the ultimate goal, peace is what you all desire, peace can be achieved but do not look towards religion for peace. Look towards yourselves, your own thoughts, your own way of living.

You can be a beacon for others as an individual.

There are many individuals who have existed, who are revered today, for their light shone.

They influenced people, they inspired people peacefully. They sought not to indoctrinate, they sought only to inspire.

They had many followers but many, many enemies but they were not speaking of religion but of peace.

Petrah (from 'A Wonderful Spiritual Journey')

Great Spirits have always encountered opposition from mediocre minds. Anyone who becomes seriously involved in the pursuit of science becomes convinced that there is a spirit manifest in the laws of the universe – a spirit vastly superior to man.

Albert Einstein

Lightning Source UK Ltd.
Milton Keynes UK
UKOW02f2309070317
296047UK00001B/88/P

9 781786 976918